The
Dictionary
of
Worthless
Words

Also by Dave Dowling

The Wrong Word Dictionary
Images of Steve Reeves
Steve Reeves: His Legacy in Films

The
Dictionary
of
Worthless
Words

3,000 Words to Stop Using Now

Dave Dowling

Marion Street Press

Portland, Oregon

Published by Marion Street Press
4207 S.E. Woodstock Blvd. # 168
Portland, OR 97206-6267
USA
http://www.marionstreetpress.com/

Orders and review copies: 800-888-4741

Printed in the United States of America

ISBN 978-1-933338-97-2
    Library of Congress Cataloging-in-Publication Data Pending

To my late and lovely wife Mary..........

Your words were *worth* so much. Thank you.

Preface

"Clutter is the disease of American writing. We are a society strangling in unnecessary words, circular constructions, big word frills, and meaningless jargon."—William Zinsser

One of the best ways to make your writing stronger is to cut unnecessary words. Many people tend to over write, and those extra words can make writing sound blurred and imprecise, rather than clear and precise. Inflated words, needless modifiers, repetition, and lengthy phrasing often litter text with many *worthless* words, thereby delaying the message. However, with exact, focused, and lively prose, audiences can get the message the first time; the verbal noise is gone. For speakers and writers who value brevity, this book was designed for you.

The Dictionary of Worthless Words is a quick reference that contains a comprehensive list of over 3,000 alphabetically listed words and phrases we can *usually* delete from our writing. For example, use the verb *investigate* instead of the diluted *perform an investigation*, or prefer *appears* over the wordy *has the appearance of*. Also, omit the tired deadwood phrases like *for all intents and purposes* or *the fact of the matter is*. Why do we make prepositional phrases out of simple verbs? We say *empty out, fill up, write down, originate from, reply back, merge together,* when the simple verbs *empty, fill, write, originate, reply,* and *merge* can typically stand alone. We also tend to over intensify words with filler phrases like *totally destroyed, completely unanimous, tiny trace,* or *small speck.* And we still use large, important-sounding words like *initialize, substantiate,* or *utilize* when small, simple words like *start, prove,* or *use* get the same result and improve the economy of the writing.

The examples in this book *suggest ways* to streamline your daily communication by identifying obvious short cuts to better communication. But this book is not intended to discourage every large word or every long phrase. Everything depends on the context of the information, and the book's recommended deletions may not always meet the intended semantic need. In those cases, leave the writing to where it will not be misinterpreted.

Some popular word padding examples may not be in this reference. For example, the legal field still accepts redundant phrases *null and void*, *last will and testament*, *terms and conditions*, and *sworn affidavit* among others. Also, the food aficionados still allow the redundant *tuna fish*, *rice paddy*, *shrimp scampi*, *chili pepper,* and *minestrone soup*. To that end, those examples are purposely not included here. But you will see *duplicate copy*, *lasting legacy*, and *grave crisis* among the countless phrases we should discard.

The old saying, "Never use two words where one will do", is still good advice. Adhere to a plain language that avoids inflated vocabulary and a convoluted sentence. Do not let the audience be distracted by communication crammed with predictable and pointless words. Let words stand alone without modifying support, and do surgery on your prose when need be. Cutting verbiage with your word scalpel can make a message simple, straightforward, and easy to understand.

As author James Kilpatrick once observed, "Paper and ink are precious, and they ought never be wasted. Conscientious writers have a duty to strike every useless word, and good writers will use no more words than are necessary to the task at hand." To that end, brevity in writing unquestionably has value, if not virtue. And, writing is more likely to be read if the reader's time is not wasted, and the words are always *worth something.*

Dave Dowling
Saratoga Springs, NY

Acknowledgments

Publishing a book requires a team effort, and few authors can successfully go it alone. Another set of eyes and another perspective can only aid in ensuring a writer's work is firm, not frail. As with my previous book, *The Wrong Word Dictionary*, I once again was surrounded by exceptional people. They were there from the beginning, and they were there to the end, always lending their valuable expertise and always giving their cooperative spirit. What a team and what a pleasure.

The team was led by the dedicated and diligent people at Marion Street Press (MSP). Their insight, guidance, and suggestions were always welcomed, always instrumental, and always appreciated. Thank you MSP for giving me another writing opportunity and for making a difference in my latest word journey. My success is certainly your success.

Also joining the effort was my former publisher, Ed Avis of Oak Park, IL. Ed and I started discussing this project way back in 2006. It was Ed who gave the initial guidance and recommendations as well as suggest the book's unique title. Thank you Ed for your endless creativity and enthusiasm, and thank you for providing the runway to get my authoring career off the ground. You were quite the considerate co-pilot.

Another key component of any publishing effort is support. The kind of support that keeps you going, keeps you focused, and keeps you encouraged about the outcome. From initial ideas to outline, from early drafts to press, my son Tim was always there to provide that continued encouragement. Thank you pal for your reassurance, for your thoughts, and for simply being whom you are. As your late mother and I said many times, "You are one exceptional son, and we were so blessed by God for His generous gift".

The
Dictionary
of
Worthless
Words

A

"Good writing can be defined as having something to say and saying it well."—Edward Abbey

abdicate
Abandon, *renounce*, or *resign* are simpler word choices.

abnormally strange
Redundant. Anything *strange* is usually *abnormal*.
She failed to notice us, which seemed ~~abnormally~~ strange.

above and beyond
Redundant prepositions. Choose one or the other but not both.
He went ~~above and~~ beyond what was required to accommodate the hotel guests.

(the) above-mentioned
This or *these* conveys the same meaning quicker.
The estimate is good only for ~~the above-mentioned~~ this work.

abrogate
Stuffy word for *annul*, *cancel*, or *repeal*.

absolute dogma, absolute fact, absolute guarantee, absolute truth, absolute necessity
Overused modifier we can typically delete.
We interpreted her opinions as ~~absolute~~ fact, not hearsay.

absolutely
Unnecessary introductory word and intensifier.
We ~~absolutely~~ believe innovation is the key to success.

Other possibilities to consider include:

absolutely awful	absolutely indispensable
absolutely certain	absolutely necessary
absolutely complete	absolutely phenomenal
absolutely conclusive	absolutely spectacular
absolutely essential	absolutely sure
absolutely incredible	absolutely vital

abundantly
Often this word can be deleted.
We made it ~~abundantly~~ clear the program is not working.

academic scholar
Redundant. *Scholars* are part of *academia*.
~~Academic~~ scholars may get aid for room, board, and tuition.

accentuate
Big verb for *highlight* or *stress*.

accidental fluke, accidental mistake
Redundant. Any *fluke* or *mistake* is accidental.
It's easy for any of us to make a simple ~~accidental~~ mistake.

accompanied by
Wordy. Try using *with* instead.
Hard rain ~~accompanied by~~ with lightning hit the area tonight.

accord respect to
Verbose. Say *respect*.
We ~~accord~~ respect ~~to~~ all persons, despite personal beliefs.

according to our data, according to our records
Hackneyed business phrases. The phrase *we find* is tighter.
~~According to our data~~ we find your file is in good order.

accordingly
Therefore or *so* are simpler and less formal words.

accounted for by the fact that

Long-winded. Try the word *because* or the phrase *caused by*.
The salary disparity is ~~accounted for by the fact that~~ because experience played a part.

accurate and factual

Verbal surplus. One of these words will do.
The diagrams in the book are ~~factual and~~ accurate.

accurate fact, accurate truth

Unneeded modifiers. *Facts* and *truths* must be accurate.
We decide, based on ~~accurate~~ facts, if a crime occurred.

accurately solve

Just say *solve*.
Her skills can ~~accurately~~ solve our quality problems.

acquiesce

Showy word for *accept*, *agree*, *comply*, or *consent*.

actions and behavior

Word overkill. Either noun will do.
They need to be accountable for their actions ~~and behavior~~.

activate, actuate

Begin or *start* say the same thing in simpler words.

active consideration

Awkward. The phrase *is considering* is more direct.
She ~~has begun active consideration of~~ is considering a presidential run.

actively engaged, actively involved

If you're *engaged* or *involved* with something, it's *active*.
The administration is ~~actively~~ engaged in fixing the dispute.
Our senior managers are ~~actively~~ involved in sales planning.

actual experience, actual fact, actual participation, actual truth

The word *actual* is an extra modifier in each phrase.
Have you had any ~~actual~~ experience in teaching physics?
The staff is in ~~actual~~ fact compensated on a daily rate.
This effort promotes the ~~actual~~ participation of everyone.
Their knowledge on the purchase is far from the ~~actual~~ truth.

actually

Often this word can be cut.
Do low-carb diets ~~actually~~ work faster than other diets?

acute crisis

Redundant. We can assume a *crisis* is *acute*.
The financial sector recovered from an ~~acute~~ crisis.

add an additional

Extra word. The word *additional* is typically not needed.
How do I add an ~~additional~~ IP address to the server?

add the point that

Filler phrase. The words *the point that* can sometimes be dropped.
Let me add ~~the point that~~, next year's budget is less.

added bonus, added extra, added perk

Extra word. The word *added* is surplus in these phrases.
As a ~~an added~~ bonus, the stock's dividend is increasing.
The car dealer offered us many ~~added~~ extras at no cost.
As ~~an added~~ perk, they gave her an expense account.

additional accessory, optional accessory

Redundant. *Accessories* are assumed to be *additional* or *optional*.
All ~~optional~~ accessory kits are shipped separately FOB.

(an) adequate number of

Wordy. The word *enough* is simpler.
We have ~~an adequate number of~~ enough votes for passage.

administrate

The word *administer* avoids the extra syllables.

admit to

Clutter. The preposition *to* is not needed here.
One competitor did admit ~~to~~ unethical practices.

admonish

Rich word for *scold*, *tell*, or *warn*.

admonition

Complex word. The word *warning* is a simpler choice.

advance

At times, the word *advance* is understood and unneeded.
Their ~~advance~~ planning certainly paid them dividends.
The residents had ~~advance~~ warning on the hurricane.

Other examples to consider include:

advance arrangement	advance preparation
advance consent	advance preview
advance forecast	advance registration
advance notice	advance reservation
advance prediction	advance scouting

advance ahead, advance forth, advance forward, advance on, advance onward

Word overkill. Use the verb *advance* by itself.
Her goal from the start was to advance ~~ahead~~ in her career.
My superiors gave an order to advance ~~forth~~ into battle.
To advance ~~forward~~, you need to complete the prerequisites.
Bob's team will easily advance ~~on~~ to the next round.
You can advance ~~onward~~ until you're told to stop.

adverse obstacle

Redundant. Any *obstacle* is *adverse* to something.
Copyright is an ~~adverse~~ obstacle plaguing some authors.

advise us as to

The phrase *let us know* is less formal.

affiliate

Inflated verb for *attach*, *join*, or *unite*.

affinity

Stuffy word for *likeness*.

(an) affirmative yes

Stuffy expression. Use the word *yes* instead.
If the answer is ~~an affirmative~~ yes, we'll start immediately.

affix your signature

Legalistic. The simple phrase *sign the paper* will do.

affluent rich

Redundant. The *rich* are the *affluent*.
Our community's ~~affluent~~ rich always support local charities.

afford an opportunity for

Long-winded. Try the words *allow*, *give*, or *let*.
~~Afford an opportunity for~~ let all sides be heard.

aforementioned

Big word. Try the simpler word *these*.

after all is said and done

Tired business cliché that's not needed.
~~After all is said and done~~ we will use the option anyway.

after careful consideration, after further consideration

Trite and tired business letter phrases. Avoid when possible.

after that has been done, after that is accomplished

Windy phrases. The word *then* can typically replace these phrases.
~~After that has been done~~ then the rule can take effect.

again

Often this is an unneeded word when following a verb.
If she's not careful, her sickness could recur ~~again~~.
To restate ~~again~~, the new process is more efficient.
The board reiterated ~~again~~ the need to adopt new measures.

Other possibilities to consider include:

reconsider again	return again
re-launch again	reuse again
remember again	revive again
repeat again	reweighed again
resume again	

Note: This advice can also apply when *again* <u>precedes</u> the verb as in *~~again~~ recur*, *~~again~~ reiterate*, *~~again~~ restate*, etc.

aggregate

Inflated noun for *sum* or *total*.

ahead of schedule

Overdone. Use the word *early* instead.
We finished the science project ~~ahead of schedule~~ early.

aid and abet, aid and assist

Repetition. The verb *aid* is plenty in either phrase.
Her actions can aid ~~and abet~~ questions of campaign money.

aim and purpose

Redundant nouns. One of these words will do.
Our ~~aim and~~ purpose is to improve the state's resources.

all across

Extra word. The word *all* is usually not needed.
Schools from ~~all~~ across the nation were present last year.

all done, all inclusive

Wordy. The word *all* is usually excess in each phrase.
When all done with the test, please review your answers.
They offer all inclusive weekly vacation package deals.

all of

Lengthy. The *of* is sometimes unneeded.
All of our children have attended state colleges.

all of a sudden

Fatty phrase. The word *suddenly* is leaner.
I rebooted and all of a sudden suddenly no PC issues.

all of the time

Chatty. The word *always* could replace this phrase.
Before taking vitamins, I was tired all of the time always.

all over again

Verbose. The word *again* could replace this phrase.
It's a dispute between the two judges all over again.

all things being equal, all things considered

Tired, padded phrases we can sometimes drop.
All things considered we are financially better today.

all-time record

Word overkill. The word *record* does not need to be qualified.
We may break our all-time record for the warmest May.

all year round

Extra word. The word *round* is unnecessary.
Where they live, they can play golf all year round.

alleged suspect

Redundant. A *suspect* is usually considered *alleged*.
The police have not yet questioned the alleged suspect.

alleviate
Hollow verb for *decrease*, *lessen*, *lighten*, or *relieve*.

allocate
Flowery word for *allot*, *give*, or *ration*.

almost all
Roundabout. *Most* is a shorter, more direct option.
Video games account for ~~almost all~~ most of their sales.

almost never
Wordy. *Seldom* is a better word choice.
The flowers ~~almost never~~ seldom bloom in March.

alone by herself
Rambling. The word *alone* is plenty.
We discovered the child was left home alone ~~by herself~~.

along the lines of
Inflated phrase for *like* or *similar to*.
This idea is ~~along the lines of~~ similar to theirs.

alongside of
Extra words. Often this phrase can be shortened to the word *along*.
The workshop I attended ran along~~side of~~ the boardwalk.

already existing
Surplus. The word *already* is not needed.
For days, we viewed many ~~already~~ existing online courses.

alter or change
Repetition. Choose one or the other but not both.
The system will not let me ~~alter or~~ change my password.

altercation
Heavy word for *dispute*, *quarrel*, or *row*.

alternative choice

Word overkill. Either word will do, but the word *choice* is simpler.
After surfing the web, we found ~~an alternative~~ a choice.

always and forever

Verbal excess. Either word will do.
We promised to support the cause always ~~and forever~~.

a.m. in the morning

Filler phrase. *In the morning* is an unneeded phrase.
A snow warning is in effect until 11 a.m. ~~in the morning~~.

ameliorate

Plush verb for *improve* or *upgrade*.

amicable

Cordial, *friendly*, or *kind* can replace this large word.

amount of

Sometimes this phrase can be cut.
Today's ~~amount of~~ credit card debt could exceed last year.

ample enough

Redundant. If something is *ample*, it's *enough*.
The low fuel demand is ~~ample~~ enough to keep prices stable.

analogous

Large word. Try the simpler words *like* or *similar*.

ancient fossil, ancient proverb, ancient relic

Extra word. The word *ancient* is excess in any of these phrases.
The ~~ancient~~ fossil was identified as a mammoth fungus.
They live their lives through many ~~ancient~~ proverbs.
The archeologist found rare artifacts and other ~~ancient~~ relics.

and additionally, and also, and moreover, and plus

Filler phrase. The conjunction *and* is plenty in all phrases.
We know little and ~~moreover~~ prefer not knowing more.

and the way in which
Verbose. The phrase *and how* is briefer.

and then
Extra word. At times, the conjunction *and* can be omitted.
The recipe batter is first mixed, ~~and~~ then poured.

annihilate
Weighty word. The verb *destroy* is simpler.

annoying and bothersome
Redundant adjectives. Choose one or the other but not both.
We found the loud music ~~annoying and~~ bothersome.

annual anniversary
Overkill. Just the word *anniversary* is plenty.
They plan on hosting the 27th ~~annual~~ anniversary dinner.

anonymous stranger
Redundant. Every *stranger* is *anonymous*.
We thanked the ~~anonymous~~ stranger for her good deeds.

another additional, another alternative
Needless modifier because *another* is implied.
We offered ~~another~~ an alternative to recycling.

antagonize
The words *annoy*, *provoke, rile*, or *upset* are simpler.

anticipate ahead, anticipate in advance
Unneeded phrase. The word *anticipate* is enough here.
Try to anticipate ~~ahead~~ some tough audience questions.
Questions are always difficult to anticipate ~~in advance~~.

any arbitrary
Word overkill. The word *arbitrary* can be cut.
Select any ~~arbitrary~~ letters or numbers for a password.

any further

Fatty phrase. The word *more* is leaner.
Can we expect ~~any further~~ more cuts to the budget?

any single one

Overdone. Drop the word *single*.
This Friday, save 20% on any ~~single~~ one clothing item.

any way, shape, or form

Tired phrase. Prefer the shorter phrase *in any way*.
Cheating in any way~~, shape, or form~~ will result in removal.

appear to be

Long-winded. At times, the word *appear* is enough.
The new university programs appear ~~to be~~ well funded.

appellation

Plush word for *label*, *name*, *tag*, *term*, or *title*.

applications and uses

Verbal excess. Either word will do.
Ascorbic acid has many industrial applications ~~and uses~~.

appointed as

Extra word. The preposition *as* is surplus.
Dr. Falk was appointed ~~as~~ the college's interim president.

appreciate in value (or worth)

Padded phrases. The phrases *in value* and *in worth* are not needed.
Her photographic prints will appreciate ~~in value~~ someday.

apprehension

Bulky noun for *fear* or *worry*.

apprise

Tell or *advise* are simpler word choices.

appropriate

Large word. Try the simpler words *apt*, *correct*, *fitting*, *proper*, *right*, or *suitable*.

approximately

Big word. The smaller words *about*, *around*, *nearly*, or *roughly* mean the same.

arbitrary

Elegant word for *chance* or *random*.

archipelago of islands

Redundant. Use the word *archipelago* alone.
The Philippines is technically an archipelago ~~of islands~~.

architecture of the building

Unneeded prepositional phrase. Use *architecture* by itself.
The architecture ~~of the building~~ resembles other designs.

are (is) in a position to

Drop this rambling expression for the verb *can.*
We ~~are in a position to~~ can recruit more people for the job.

are (is) in agreement with

Stale phrase. Try using the word *agree* by itself.
On the issue of fairness, we ~~are in agreement~~ agree.

are (is) in possession of

Muddle. The simple verbs *has*, *have*, or *own* will do.
We ~~are in possession of~~ have two tickets to the opera.

are (is) in receipt of

Rambling. Use the verbs *have* or *received* instead.
We ~~are in receipt of~~ have your transcript request.

are indications of

Extra words. At times, the verb *indicate* is crisper.
Sinus pains ~~are indications of~~ indicate harsh climate change.

are (is) intended to

Windy. Often this phrase can be cut.

These golf clubs ~~are intended to~~ give you more accuracy.

are (is) known to be

Chatty. This phrase can be trimmed to the word *are*.

Fossil carbonate skeletons are ~~known to be~~ well preserved.

are (is) of the same opinion

Stale phrase. The simple verb *agree* carries the same meaning.

We ~~are of the same opinion~~ agree things need to improve.

are (is) provided with

Wasteful. The verb *have* can replace this phrase.

All attendees ~~are provided with~~ have dining hall privileges.

are (is) required to

Padded phrase. The verb *must* can say the same thing.

The visitors ~~are required to~~ must show a form of ID.

are (is) situated

Extra word. The verb *situated* can often be dropped.

All preferred hotels are ~~situated~~ within walking distance.

are (is) structured to provide

Wordy. The verb *provide* can replace this phrase.

Investments ~~are structured to~~ provide liquidity within seven years.

are (is) suggestive of

Verbose. The verb *suggest* is more concise.

The discolorations ~~are suggestive of~~ suggest sun damage.

are then further

Chatty. The verb phrase *will be* is shorter.

Businesses ~~are then further~~ will be classified in each division.

arguably

Unneeded word. It typically adds little to a sentence.
They are ~~arguably~~ the two best players in the league.

armed gunman, armed holdup

Redundant. All *gunmen* and *holdups* are *armed*.
The police are in a standoff with ~~an~~ ~~armed~~ gunman.
They know exactly what to do if ~~an~~ ~~armed~~ holdup occurs.

arrange to return

Rambling. The verb *return* is crisper.
Contact them to ~~arrange to~~ return the product for a refund.

arrive at a conclusion

Overblown. Use the verb *conclude*.
The scientists may ~~arrive at a conclusion~~ conclude early.

arrive at a decision

Roundabout. The verbs *decide* or *reach* are more concise.
It takes 12 jurors to ~~arrive at a decision~~ decide.

articulate

Complex verb. The verb *explain* is simpler.

artificial prosthesis

Redundant. A *prosthesis* is an *artificial* limb.
Metal alloys are often used in making ~~an~~ ~~artificial~~ prosthesis.

as a consequence

Verbose. The phrase *because of* is a little more direct.
~~As a consequence~~ because of warming, ice caps are melting.

as a last resort

Empty phrase we can usually omit.
~~As a last resort~~ we could reinstall the operating system.

as a matter of fact

Extra words. Often this phrase can be cut.
As a matter of fact we will be at the conference tonight.

as a means to

Long-winded. The words *for* or *to* are shorter.
We went to four dealers as a means to get the best price.

as a person

Pointless phrase. Many times this phrase can be cut.
As a person I resent that attitude toward others.

as a result of

Verbose. The phrase *because of* is shorter.
The flood occurred as a result because of a levee breaking.

as a rule

Wordy. The words *typically* or *usually* carry the same meaning.
As a rule usually we do not comment on any allegations.

as a way to

Lengthy. The word *to* is a simpler choice.
We researched six hotels as a way to get the best price.

as a whole

This phrase adds little to any sentence.
The corporation as a whole did well on the customer survey.

as far as I am concerned

Rambling. Use the phrase *I believe*.
As far as I am concerned I believe eight hours of sleep is plenty.

as for example

Wordy. *As* is an unnecessary word.
Cars can have musical names, as for example the Sonata.

as it is now apparent

Long-winded. The word *apparently* could replace this phrase.
As it is now apparent apparently we were misinformed.

as long as, so long as

The word *if* can typically replace these wordy phrases.
The outdoor event will go on ~~as long as~~ if the weather holds.

as of this date, as of this time, as of today

Wordy. Try using the words *currently* or *today* instead.
~~As of this date~~ currently we have not received our order.

as of yet

Needless phrase.
Her latest novel is ~~as of yet~~ unfinished and unedited.

as per our agreement, as per our conversation, as per your request

Trite business letter phrases. Avoid if possible.

as regards, as related to

Empty phrases. Use the preposition *about*.
Is he optimistic or pessimistic ~~as regards~~ about the future?
What's their position ~~as related to~~ about God and religion?

as soon as

Clutter. The word *when* is more concise.
Please respond to our invitation ~~as soon as~~ when possible.

as to whether

Overkill. Just the word *whether* is enough.
The class argued ~~as to~~ whether glass is a liquid or solid.

as well as

Word excess. The words *and* or *also* can replace this phrase.
We will expand venture capital ~~as well as~~ and incentives.

as you are aware

Stale business phrase. Try replacing this phrase with the word *yes*.
~~As you are aware~~ yes, the winners are notified immediately.

ascertain

Large verb for *check*, *discover*, *find*, or *learn*.

ask a question, ask for help

Repetition. The word *ask* by itself is plenty.
Before you ask ~~a question~~, read the entire brochure.
If you need specific directions, please ask ~~for help~~.

assembled in a group

Often the phrase *in a group* is surplus.
The students assembled ~~in a group~~ in the auditorium.

assimilate

Overblown verb for *absorb*, *gather*, or *learn*.

assistance

The verbs *aid* or *help* are more modest.

associated with

The simple word *of* can sometimes replace this stilted phrase.
We know the ergonomic effects ~~associated with~~ of keyboards.

assortment

The words *mix* or *variety* are simpler word choices.

assuming that

Rambling way to say *if*.
You will lose weight, ~~assuming that~~ if you exercise and diet.

assures that all

The verb *guarantees* is much crisper.
It ~~assures that all~~ guarantees reservations will be honored.

at

Avoid ending a sentence with this redundant preposition.
Where is the meeting being held ~~at~~?
Where is she ~~at~~?

Note: At times, ending a sentence with *at* is okay.
What are you looking at?

at a later date, at a later time

The word *later* can replace these time-consuming phrases.
Still photos can be taken from the video ~~at a~~ later ~~time~~.

at a point

At times, this padded phrase can be dropped.
We are living ~~at a point~~ 500 feet below sea level.

at a price of

The word *for* can replace this tedious phrase.
The coat was advertised ~~at a price of~~ for $100.

at about

We can do without the word *at* in this context.
We leave for work each day ~~at~~ about 7.

at all times

Padded phrasing. Use the word *always*.
To be safe, you need to wear the seatbelt ~~at all times~~ always.

at an early date

Long-winded. Try the words *early* or *soon*.
They recommend you apply for the position ~~at an~~ early ~~date~~.

at present

Chatty. Use the word *now*.
She is out of the office ~~at present~~ now and will return later.

at regular intervals of time

Long-winded. Try the word *regularly*.
The medication is given ~~at regular intervals of time~~ *regularly.*

at some future date, at some time to come

Inflated phrasing. Use the words *sometime* or *later*.
We expect cable service to that city ~~at some future date~~ *later.*

at some point in time, at that point in time, at this point in time

Jargon. The words *sometime*, *then*, and *now* are shorter.
We realized luck would end sometime ~~at some point in time.~~
~~At that point in time~~ *then, we will discuss all our options.*
Though I cannot help you ~~at this point in time~~ *now, I will later.*

at the completion of, at the conclusion of

Filler phrases. The word *after* is simpler.
~~At the completion of~~ *after this seminar, we are free to go.*
I will recap the minutes after ~~at the conclusion of~~ *the meeting.*

at the end of the day

Tired, overused phrase. Try *in the end* instead.
~~At the end of the day~~ *in the end, I need more data for the task.*

at the present time, at this juncture

Complex way to say *now*.
HD TV is available ~~at the present time~~ *now.*
~~At this juncture~~ *now economic forecasting is only a guess.*

at the rate of

Padded phrase. Just the word *at* is plenty.
Vacation accrues at ~~the rate of~~ *two working days a month.*

at your earliest convenience

A stale business phrase. Try using the phrase *as soon as*.
Apply ~~at your earliest convenience~~ *as soon as possible.*

atop of

Omit the useless preposition *of*.
The school board is atop ~~of~~ the situation.

attached hereto, attached herewith, attached please find

Business letter clichés. Go with the verb *attached*.
Attached ~~herewith~~ is the letter I wrote to the administrator.

attest to the fact that

Tedious. The words *show* or *prove* can often mean the same.
I can ~~attest to the fact that~~ show all proceeds went to charity.

attire

Big word. Try the simpler word *dress.*

attractive in appearance

Needless ending phrase.
Compared to other wood finishes, oak is attractive ~~in appearance~~.

attribute (as a noun)

Big word for the simpler words *feature*, *quality*, or *trait.*

attribute (as a verb)

Lush word for *assign* or *credit.*

auction sale

Redundant. An *auction* is a *sale*.
To raise money this year, we're having a public auction ~~sale~~.

(an) audible gasp, audible to the ear

Word overkill. Use the words *gasp* or *audible*.
~~An audible~~ a gasp was clearly heard after his remarks.
The CD's slight skip was clearly audible ~~to the ear~~.

audio sound system

Redundant. The word *audio* is not needed.
The car's ~~audio~~ sound system is easy to install.

augment

Prefer the simpler verbs *boost*, *enlarge*, or *increase*.

authentic

The simple words *real* or *true* carry the same meaning.

authentic replica

Redundant. *Replica* implies being *authentic*.
Obviously a skilled craftsman made this ~~authentic~~ replica.

authorize

Large verb for the simpler verbs *allow* or *permit*.

(an) automatic habit

Redundant. If it is a *habit*, it is *automatic*.
My car has an ~~automatic~~ habit of stalling in the cold.

(the) autumn season

Redundant. It's implied *autumn* is a *season*.
Our leaves turn colors early in ~~the~~ autumn ~~season~~.

auxiliary

Elegant word for *added*, *extra*, or *spare*.

avail yourself

The simple verb *use* says the same thing.
You should ~~avail yourself~~ use the opportunity to buy stock.

average about, debate about, know about

The preposition *about* is excess in all these phrases.
We typically average ~~about~~ 20 business trips a year.
They will debate ~~about~~ genetic engineering for days.
Here are beneficial things you may need to know ~~about~~.

away

Often a pointless word, especially when preceded by a verb or followed by *from*.

The attention was diverted ~~away~~ from their unfortunate gaffes.
The sand will erode ~~away~~ faster from unprotected areas.
They now live farther ~~away~~ from work than they used to.
The animals were isolated ~~away~~ from the general public.
Surprisingly, she now shifted ~~away~~ from her initial position.

Other examples to consider include:

clean away	melt away
clear away	migrate away
cut away	move away
deflect away	run away
drift away	send away
empty away	separate away
fade away	sequester away
file away	take away
flush away	turn away
give away	walk away
hammer away	wash away
look away	whittle away
march away	wrote away

away from

Sometimes *away* is an unessential modifying preposition.
We are years ~~away~~ from solving our energy problems.

awesome

A tired, overused word that people use incorrectly as meaning *great* or *impressive*. The word technically means *inspiring awe*. Avoid its improper use.

awful bad

Repetition. Choose one or the other but not both.
We felt awful ~~bad~~ about his rejection from medical school.

(an) awkward predicament
Redundant. Any *predicament* is *awkward*.
Forgetting your own birthday is ~~an~~ awkward ~~predicament~~.

axiomatic
Heavy word for *clear* or *obvious*.

B

"Reading makes a full man; conference a ready man; and writing an exact man."—Sir Francis Bacon

baby calf, baby kid, baby puppy

Redundant modifiers. The word *baby* is surplus.

back

Back is usually a needless ending preposition when it follows a verb.
Please wait until we arrive ~~back~~ home later tonight.
The fugitive was finally extradited ~~back~~ to New York last month.
She immediately heard ~~back~~ from the company about the job.
After the turn, the road will loop ~~back~~ around to the highway.
Both groups can relate ~~back~~ to the experience of raising children.
Please write ~~back~~ when your schedule is free.

Other possibilities to consider include:

add back	relay back
call back	remand back
cut back	remember back
dates back	remit back
defer back	repay back
disperse back	repeat back
drift back	reply back
echo back	report back
funnel back	respond back
pay back	restore back
rebound back	retreat back
recall back	return back
recede back	reverse back
receive back	revert back
recite back	send back
recoil back	shift back
refer back	stretch back
reflect back	trace back
regress back	transfer back

back to the drawing board
Overused business cliché. The phrase *start again* is fresher.

background of experience
Redundant. A *background* of something implies *experience*.
Her ~~background of~~ experience included years as a teacher.

bad evil, bad trouble, bad vices
Drop *bad*. It's understood these things are all *bad*.
The Mars rover experienced ~~bad~~ trouble on its recent trip.

balance against one another, balance evenly
Overstated. The verb *balance* will do for both phrases.
The diet suggests both food groups be balanced ~~evenly~~.

bald headed
Word overkill. The word *headed* is unnecessary.
Some people find bald ~~headed~~ people attractive.

ball's in your court
Tired cliché. Avoid.

ballpark figure
Tired cliché that could be replaced with the noun *estimate*.
We need a(n) ~~ballpark figure~~ estimate for the new city building.

bare naked
The word *bare* is unnecessary.
The victim was found ~~bare~~ naked by the road.

barracks building
Redundant. The word *barracks* implies a *building*.
At one time, the barracks ~~building~~ served as a hospital.

based in large part on
Chatty. Try simply *based mainly on*.
Their success is based ~~in large part~~ mainly on revenues.

based on the conclusion that, based on the fact that

Long-winded. Pare these phrases to simply *because*.

~~Based on the fact that,~~ *because you're not on the plan now, your coverage expired.*

baseless rumor, unconfirmed rumor, unfounded rumor, unsubstantiated rumor

Redundant. *Rumors* are always *baseless, unconfirmed,* or *unsubstantiated.*

The report was false and viewed as a ~~baseless~~ rumor.
~~Unconfirmed~~ *rumors report PCs will see price cuts this year.*
~~Unfounded~~ *rumors about the company sale were rampant.*
The ~~unsubstantiated~~ rumor started right after he left politics.

basic and fundamental

Redundant adjectives. Use the word *basic*.
The attorney explained their basic ~~and fundamental~~ rights.

basic essential, basic fundamental, basic gist, basic necessity, basic principle

Redundant modifiers. The word *basic* is implied.
The tutorial helped us get the ~~basic~~ gist of the program.

basically, more or less

Extra words. These phrases often can be deleted.
To say hybrid cars are not selling well is ~~basically~~ untrue.
The software is becoming ~~more or less~~ obsolete.

be aware of, is aware of, was aware of

Rambling. The verb *knows* is more precise.
The community ~~is aware of~~ knows the risk of skin cancer.

be cognizant of, be familiar with

Clutter. Use the word *know*.
Tenants should ~~be familiar with~~ know their obligations.

be deficient in

Wordy. The word *lack* is a simpler replacement
Many patients may be deficient in lack vitamin D.

be in accord

Long-winded. Use the verb *agree*.
The hotel must be in accord agree with the building codes.

be of the opinion

Diluted phrase for *believe*.
He could be of the opinion believe the cost is too high now.

be that as it may

Needless phrase. Go with *anyhow*, *still*, or *yet*.
Be that as it may still, I overreacted to the situation.

bear a grudge against

Long-winded. The words *dislike* or *resent* are crisper.
They bear a grudge against dislike next week's opponents.

bear in mind

The words *consider*, *heed*, *note*, or *realize* are shorter.
Bear in mind realize that few companies lack websites.

bears a resemblance to

Verbose. Use the verb *resembles*.
His writing bears a resemblance to resembles Tom Clancy's.

because of the fact that, due to the fact that, given the fact that

Tiresome phrases. Try the words *because* or *considering*.
I was late because of the fact that I had wrong directions.
Due to the fact that because it rained, I delayed the game.
Given the fact that considering the weather, let's postpone.

become cognizant

Stuffy. Use the word *know*.
In business, you must become cognizant know the customer.

beg to differ
Rambling. Use the verb *disagree*.
We ~~beg to differ~~ disagree with the judge's questionable ruling.

begin and commence
Repetitive and wordy. The word *start* can replace this phrase.
The project will ~~begin and commence~~ start on May 1.

being placed
Verbal surplus. An expression we can often omit.
The diet has an emphasis ~~being placed~~ on less red meat.

beneficial
Hefty adjective for *good*, *helpful,* or *useful*.

beneficial aspects
The noun *benefits* is much crisper.
We are studying the ~~beneficial aspects~~ benefits of the drug.

beside the point
Roundabout. The words *immaterial*, *irrelevant*, or *unrelated* are more direct.
Whether you have insurance is ~~beside the point~~ irrelevant.

between the two of them
Excess. The phrase *between them* is plenty here.
Between ~~the two of~~ them, they accounted for the entire score.

between you and me
Verbose. The phrase *between us* is shorter.
Between ~~you and me~~ us, we cannot ignore this great offer.

beverage
The word *drink* means the same and is simpler.

beyond a (the) shadow of a doubt
Long phrase. Try *certainly*, *obviously*, *surely*, or *undoubtedly*.
It proves ~~beyond a shadow of a doubt~~ surely his innocence.

beyond the realm of possibility

Roundabout. Words like *impossible* or *inconceivable* are more direct.

It's ~~beyond the realm of possibility~~ impossible that he is guilty.

biased opinion

Word overkill. Go with *bias*.

He expressed a bias~~ed opinion~~ about the recent decision.

big, huge/big, large

Word overkill. The word *big* is not needed.

They now live in a ~~big,~~ huge house outside of Boston.

bisect into two parts

Overstated. The word *bisect* alone is plenty.

The new train track will bisect the road ~~into two parts~~.

bits and pieces

Redundant nouns. Either word will do.

The tornado left the town in ~~bits and~~ pieces.

bitter disappointment

Redundant. *Disappointments* are assumed to be *bitter*.

Not being interviewed for the job was a ~~bitter~~ disappointment.

blatantly obvious

Redundant. If it's *obvious*, it's *blatant*.

Their attempt to influence the elections was ~~blatantly~~ obvious.

blend of both

On occasion, the word *both* is unnecessary.

The drink consisted of a blend of ~~both~~ apples and oranges.

bloated verbiage

Unneeded modifier.

She expels volumes of ~~bloated~~ verbiage in a speech.

blood hemorrhage

Redundant. All *hemorrhages* contain *blood*.
After the fall, he was diagnosed with a ~~blood~~ hemorrhage.

blue-sky thinking

Tired cliché. Try to avoid.

boat marina

Redundant. A *marina* pertains to *boats*.
This summer the town ~~boat~~ marina has many vacant slips.

bode well for the future

Extra words. The phrase *bode well* is plenty.
Today's economic climate may not bode well ~~for the future~~.

boiling hot

Redundant. Anything *boiling* is *hot*.
The park has boiling ~~hot~~ springs alongside serene lakes.

boisterous

Lively, *noisy*, or *rowdy* can replace this large word.

(a) bolt of lightning

The phrase *a bolt of* can be cut.
~~A bolt of~~ lightning struck her while on the golf course.

borrowed loan

Redundant. Any *loan* is *borrowed*.
After May 1, the interest rate for ~~borrowed~~ loans will be 6.8%.

both alike

Often the word *alike* by itself is enough.
The two colleges are ~~both~~ alike in their areas of study.

both equally, both share

The word *both* is unnecessary.
The dinner recipes were ~~both~~ equally delicious.
They ~~both~~ share a deep commitment to the poor.

both of them, both of these

The word *both* by itself is enough.
Both of them subscribe to Time *and* Newsweek *magazines.*
Recent findings challenge both of these scientific theories.

bothersome and annoying

Redundant adjectives. Choose one or the other but not both.
We found the loud music bothersome and annoying.

bound and determined

Verbal overload. The word *determined* will do.
Joe was bound and determined to see his song recorded.

bouquet of flowers

Needless ending phrase. *Bouquets* are *flowers.*
She received a bouquet of flowers for Valentine's Day.

brand new

The word *new* by itself is enough.
The station features brand new videos, music, and news.

brand-new beginner

Redundant. Usually *beginners* are *brand-new.*
This class teaches brand-new beginners the basics of yoga.

brave and courageous

Redundant adjectives. Choose one or the other but not both.
Unlike others, she is brave and courageous to try.

breaking and entering

Redundant verbs. Choose one verb or the other.
The accused was seen breaking and entering the house.

brief cameo, brief glance, brief moment, brief overview, brief respite, brief spasm, brief summary, brief synopsis

Overstated. The word *brief* is already implied.
Alfred Hitchcock has made ~~brief~~ cameos in his own films.
The speaker needed only a ~~brief~~ glance at his material.
Please take a ~~brief~~ moment to complete this course survey.
Today we're giving a ~~brief~~ overview to the team.
The partisanship returned to Washington after a ~~brief~~ respite.
Laryngo is a ~~brief~~ spasm of the vocal cords.
You need to give a ~~brief~~ summary to the customers.
The essay is intended as a ~~brief~~ synopsis of the novel.

briefly in passing

The phrase *in passing* is not needed.
Let me say briefly ~~in passing~~ that the class went well.

bring to a conclusion, bring to an end, bring to a halt

Long-winded. Use the verbs *conclude*, *end*, or *halt*.
I am going to ~~bring to a conclusion~~ conclude this long debate.
We are hoping to ~~bring to an~~ end the week-long negotiations.
The workload decision could ~~bring to a~~ halt new hiring.

brings to mind

The verbs *recalls* or *suggests* are simpler.
His style ~~brings to mind~~ recalls a player from another era.

broad daylight

Excess modifier. *Daylight* implies *broad*.
The security guard saw a laptop stolen in ~~broad~~ daylight.

brusque

The words *abrupt*, *brisk*, *curt*, or *rough* carry the same meaning.

(a) bunch of

Often it's simpler to say the word *many*.
We found ~~a bunch of~~ many students liked the night class.

burning hot embers

Redundant. *Embers* are *burning hot*.
She stayed by the fire until the ~~burning hot~~ embers faded.

but however, but nevertheless, but yet

Repetition. The word *but* by itself is plenty.
She applied for student aid, but ~~however~~ it may be too late.
It's a lesser known but ~~nevertheless~~ important disease.
He advises on health matters, but ~~yet~~ he still smokes.

but there are other.....that

At times, *but other* can replace this phrase.
But ~~there are~~ other products ~~that~~ work as well.

by a factor of two

The words *double*, *twice*, or *two times* are more concise.
We increased our sales ~~by a factor of~~ two times.

Note: The same guideline could apply to other numerical values
(*by a factor of <u>three</u>*, *by a factor of <u>four</u>*, etc.).

by and large

Tedious. The word *usually* can often replace this phrase.
~~By and large~~ usually our weekly meetings are productive.

by means of, by the use of, by virtue of, by way of

Windy phrases. Try using *by*, *through*, or *with* instead.
Forests are coming back ~~by means of~~ through preservation.
He reduced energy loss ~~by the use of~~ with new windows.
The economy improved by ~~virtue of~~ lowering many taxes.
We typically travel to Utica by ~~way of~~ Interstate 81.

by reason of the fact, by virtue of the fact that

The word *because* can replace these long phrases.
I didn't attend ~~by reason of the fact that~~ because it rained.

by the same token

A cliché easily replaced with *likewise*, *moreover*, *similarly*, etc.
You should respect your colleagues, and ~~by the same token~~ similarly they should respect you.

by way of comparison, by way of contrast

The words *but*, *however*, *whereas*, or *yet* can replace these phrases.
Harvard was established in 1636; ~~by way of comparison~~, whereas William and Mary was established in 1693.
~~By way of contrast~~ however, this car gets 35 miles to the gallon.

by way of example, by way of illustration

Phrases like *for example* or *to illustrate* are more concise.
~~By way of~~ for example, he noted the quirks of translating French into English.
~~By way of illustration,~~ to illustrate, the builder showed us how the house would look on the lot.

C

"Broadly speaking, the short words are the best, and the old words when short are best of all."—Winston Churchill

cabal of people

Redundant. A *cabal* can only be *people*.
A small cabal ~~of people~~ in the government made the decisions.

cacophony of sound

Redundant. A *cacophony* is a *sound*.
We heard a cacophony ~~of sound~~ coming from the cafeteria.

call a halt to, call a stop to, call an end to

Wordy. The verbs *halt*, *stop*, or *end* are shorter.
~~Call a halt to~~ halt all activity on the new contract.
He wants to ~~call a~~ stop ~~to~~ the domestic spying program.
The minister wants to ~~call an~~ end ~~to~~ the violence now.

call your attention to the fact that

Long-winded. Trim this phrase to simply *remind you*.
I ~~call your attention to the fact that~~ remind you it's due today.

called upon and asked

Overstated. Use the phrase *called upon*.
Engineers were called upon ~~and asked~~ for safety issues.

calls for

Rambling. A better option is the word *requires*.
The recipe ~~calls for~~ requires one tablespoon of a dried herb.

came at a time when

Delete the phrase *at a time*.
Our bonuses came ~~at a time~~ when we needed them.

came to a realization

Chatty. Use the verb *realized*.
He ~~came to a realization~~ realized how lucky he was to be alive.

came to a stop

Long-winded. Try the verb *stopped*.
Once the power failed, all systems ~~came to a stop~~ stopped.

came to an abrupt end

Excess. The phrase *abruptly ended* is simpler.
The peace talks ~~came to an abrupt end~~ abruptly ended.

came to an agreement

Verbose. Use the verb *agreed*.
The owners ~~came to an agreement~~ agreed on the salary caps.

cameo appearance

Redundant. A *cameo* is an *appearance*.
Alfred Hitchcock did a cameo ~~appearance~~ in that film.

can be seen as

Chatty. The word *is* can replace this phrase.
This ~~can be seen as~~ is a book for Internet novices.

cannot and will not

Repetition. Choose one or the other but not both.
They cannot ~~and will not~~ accept this latest policy decision.

capacious

Big word for the simpler words *big*, *huge*, *large*, or *roomy*.

capital city

Excess. The word *city* can be dropped.
G. Washington is the namesake for the capital ~~city~~ of the U.S.

Capitol building

Extra word. The word *building* is not needed.
The granite on the Capitol ~~building~~ glows like a beacon.

capitulate

Cede, *submit*, *surrender*, or *yield* are simpler word choices.

careful and cautious

Redundant adjectives. Choose one or the other but not both.
Be careful ~~and cautious~~ about accepting the right job offer.

careful consideration, careful scrutiny, close scrutiny

Redundant. *Consideration* and *scrutiny* imply being *careful* or *close*.
After ~~careful~~ consideration, the oil drilling will cease this year.
Any new equipment purchases are requiring ~~careful~~ scrutiny.
The board pressed for ~~close~~ scrutiny of the proposed merger.

careless error

Verbal surplus. *Errors* are often *careless*.
The committee made ~~a careless~~ an error in the vote counting.

carport shelter

Redundant. A *carport* is a *shelter*.
For now, the trucks are parked in a carport ~~shelter~~.

carry out an evaluation of, carry out the experiment

The verbs *evaluate* or *experiment* say the same thing.
Her staff will ~~carry out an evaluation of~~ evaluate the process.
How do you propose we ~~carry out the~~ experiment today?

carry out the order

The verb *obey* is briefer.
They expect everyone to ~~carry out the orders~~ obey.

cascading waterfall

Redundant. *Waterfalls* always *cascade*.
The high ~~cascading~~ waterfall surrounds the lush vegetation.

catapulted forward

Redundant. *Catapulted* means going *forward*.
The seat belt stops you from being catapulted ~~forward~~.

caused due to

Repetition. Use *caused* or *due to* but not both.
The fire was ~~caused~~ due to a faulty electrical circuit.

caused injury to

Shortened this phrase to the word *injured*.
The flat tire ~~caused injury to~~ injured the passengers.

cease and desist

The word *stop* says the same thing.
After May 1, all the project work will ~~cease and desist~~ stop.

certainly

This qualifier seldom adds anything.
We ~~certainly~~ agree with them on this strategic issue.

changes or alterations

Redundant nouns. Either word will do.
Changes ~~or alterations~~ can only be made within 30 days.

characteristic

The simpler word *trait* carries the same meaning.

characterize

The verb *describe* is more concise.

cheap and inexpensive

Redundant adjectives. Choose one or the other but not both.
A cheap ~~and inexpensive~~ service hosts our website.

check into, infiltrate into, penetrate into, probe into

At times, the preposition *into* is unnecessary.
We first want to check ~~into~~ the building's safety record.
The clay soil did not let the water infiltrate ~~into~~ the ground.
Solar radiation can penetrate ~~into~~ the Earth's atmosphere.
The investigator felt no need to probe ~~into~~ more evidence.

check on

Sometimes the word *on* is not needed.
I asked her to check ~~on~~ the candidate's background.

chief protagonist

The word *chief* is unnecessary.
In the novel Ulysses, *the ~~chief~~ protagonist is Leopold Bloom.*

circle around, circulate around, scatter around

Sometimes *around* is a needless ending preposition.
The tour boat is scheduled to circle ~~around~~ Liberty Island.
A new PC virus started to circulate ~~around~~ through email.
Various beautiful stone bridges scatter ~~around~~ the city.

circular shaped

The word *shaped* is not always essential to the meaning.
He made a photo-mosaic of five circular ~~shaped~~ images.

circumspect

Careful or *cautious* are simpler words.

circumvent

Avoid, *dodge*, *prevent*, or *skirt* are simpler word choices.

clap with both hands

The word *clap* is plenty.
To stay in rhyme, the children clapped ~~with both hands~~.

classify into groups

The phrase *into groups* is excess.
Taxonomy involves classifying organisms ~~into groups~~.

clearly apparent, clearly articulate, clearly evident

Clearly is a redundant modifier in all these examples.
From her grades, it's ~~clearly~~ apparent she studied.
The candidate can ~~clearly~~ articulate her points.
It's ~~clearly~~ evident we did not prepare enough.

clench tightly

Overdone. The word *clench* is plenty.
The dentist asked her to clench her teeth ~~tightly~~.

close proximity

The word *proximity* by itself is plenty.
Consider the ~~close~~ *proximity of their two adjacent houses.*

closed fist

Redundant. Every *fist* is *closed*.
The volleyball rules let you serve with a ~~closed~~ *fist.*

closely adjoining

Redundant. If it's *adjoining*, it's *close*.
The team arranged for ~~closely~~ *adjoining hotel rooms.*

closely guarded secret

Redundant. All *secrets* are assumed to be *closely guarded*.
That organization has many ~~closely guarded~~ *secrets.*

coercion

Big word for the simpler word *force*.

cognizant

Aware, *knowing*, or *mindful* are simpler words.

cold frost, cold ice

Redundant. *Frost* and *ice* are assumed to be *cold*.
The beverages are packed in a cooler of ~~cold~~ *ice.*
The unexpected ~~cold~~ *frost damaged many of the crops.*

combined total

The word *combined* is surplus.
They have a ~~combined~~ *total of 40 years IT experience.*

come into conflict

Usually the verb *conflict* is plenty.
Certain groups ~~come into~~ *conflict over the death penalty.*

come to an end

Long-winded. The word *end* will work.
All good things must ~~come to an~~ end sometime.

comfortable with, consult with, meet with, suffer with, visit with

The word *with* is rarely needed in these phrases.
He's still not comfortable ~~with~~ working out of town.
Anyone with this illness should consult ~~with~~ a physician.
The delegates will meet ~~with~~ the Prime Minister today.
Many young adults suffer ~~with~~ migraine headaches.
The English class will visit ~~with~~ the renowned author next week.

coming to terms with

Roundabout. The word *accepting* is more direct.
We are finally ~~coming to terms with~~ accepting the outcome.

comings and goings

The word *travels* is crisper.
During your ~~comings and goings~~ travels, please stop by.

commence

Complex verb for *begin* or *start*.

commensurate

Big word for the simpler words *equal* or *matching*.

common bond, common similarities

The word *common* is typically not needed.
We formed a ~~common~~ bond with the board members.
We have many ~~common~~ similarities between the groups.

commute back and forth

Repetition. Omit the phrase *back and forth*.
They commute ~~back and forth~~ to work by train.

compare and contrast

Redundant verbs. One of these words will do.
The doctors will compare ~~and contrast~~ the two diets.

compare them to one another

Needless ending phrase.
We compared them ~~to one another~~ for many reasons.

compensate, compensation

Heavy verbs and nouns for the much simpler word *pay*.

compete against each other, compete with each other

Word overkill. The word *compete* is enough in both phrases.
Colleges compete ~~against each other~~ for certain students.
Animals compete ~~with each other~~ for the same food source.

compiled compendium

Excess modifier. *Compendiums* are assumed to be *compiled*.
We bought a ~~compiled~~ compendium of celebrity TV trivia.

complete

Unneeded qualifier when the word is already implied.
The investors formed a ~~complete~~ monopoly in real estate.
The fire turned the house into a ~~complete~~ ruin.
Her promotion to president was a ~~complete~~ surprise to many.

Other examples to consider include:

complete confidence
complete finish
complete master
complete stop

complete stranger
complete total
complete unanimity

complete and full, complete and total, complete and utter

Extra words. Either word will do in each phrase.
The glossary contains a ~~complete and~~ full description.
The company agreed to issue a complete ~~and total~~ refund.
Looking back, Tim's career was a complete ~~and utter~~ success.

completely

Unneeded qualifier when the word is already implied.

The city hall was ~~completely~~ *destroyed by fire.*

By noon, the theater was ~~completely~~ *filled.*

They're trying to ~~completely~~ *eradicate computer viruses.*

Other possibilities to consider include:

completely abolish	completely full
completely accurate	completely ignore
completely annihilate	completely infinite
completely blind	completely liquidate
completely certain	completely lost
completely compatible	completely omnipotent
completely consistent	completely opposite
completely covered	completely pure
completely deaf	completely separate
completely demolish	completely sure
completely devoid	completely surround
completely devoted	completely through
completely eliminate	completely unabridged
completely empty	completely unanimous
completely engulf	completely unified
completely equal	completely unique
completely expire	completely worthless
completely finish	

comply with

The words *follow* or *obey* can replace this phrase.

This brochure can help you ~~comply with~~ *follow the new rules.*

(the) composition of

At times, this phrase can be omitted.

~~*The composition of*~~ *the team experience level is nine years.*

comprehensive

Big word for the simpler words *broad*, *complete*, or *thorough*.

conceptual idea

Redundant. *Ideas* come from *concepts*.
They asked for ~~conceptual~~ ideas that were innovative.

conceptualization

Overly complex. Use the simpler nouns *draft*, *idea*, or *plan*.

concern and interest

Double nouns. Either word will do.
We appreciate your concern ~~and interest~~ for our family.

concerning the matter of, regarding the matter of

Verbose. Use the word *about*.
My point ~~concerning the matter of~~ about him is unchanged.
More data ~~regarding the matter of~~ about the company is online.

concise overview, concise summary, concise synopsis

Overstated. These words already imply something *concise*.
Today she's giving a(n) ~~concise~~ overview to the class.
He needs to give a ~~concise~~ summary to the customers.
The report is intended as a ~~concise~~ synopsis of the novel.

conclude at the end of

Unessential ending phrase.
The trial will conclude ~~at the end of~~ this month.

conclusive proof

Redundant. *Proof* is always *conclusive*.
We have ~~conclusive~~ proof the accused is innocent.

concurrence

Big word for the simpler word *consent*.

condensed summary

Overstated. A *summary* is always a *condensed* version.
This article is a ~~condensed~~ summary from her research paper.

conduct a review of, conduct an analysis of, conduct an investigation of, conduct an experiment

Wordy phrases. Try the verbs *review*, *analyze*, *investigate*, or *experiment*.

We will ~~conduct a~~ review ~~of~~ the flyer right before publication.
He will ~~conduct an analysis of~~ analyze the customer feedback.
She will ~~conduct an investigation of~~ investigate the evidence.
I will ~~conduct an experiment~~ experiment using their methods.

confessed and acknowledged

Redundant verbs. One of these words will do.
They ~~confessed and~~ acknowledged their planning errors.

confidential

Showy word for *private* or *secret.*

configuration

Design, *form*, *pattern*, or *shape* are simpler word choices.

conjecture

Heavy word for *guess*, *theory*, or *think*.

consciously aware

Unessential modifier. You must be *conscious* to be *aware*.
At what age are children ~~consciously~~ aware of world events?

consecutive days (weeks, months, years, etc.) in a row

Drop the unneeded phrase *in a row*.
It rained for 10 consecutive days ~~in a row~~.

consecutive straight

Repetition. Use either *consecutive* or *straight* but not both.
She won her third consecutive ~~straight~~ golf tournament.

consensus of opinion

Redundant. *Consensus* implies *opinion*.
What is the consensus ~~of opinion~~ regarding the new rules.

consequence

The words *outcome* or *result* are simpler.

consequent results

Needless modifier.

~~Consequent~~ results are key to determining the cause.

consequently

Plush word. Use the words *so* or *thus*.

(a) considerable amount of, considerable number of, considerable portion of

The words *most* or *much* can replace these long phrases.

He spends ~~a considerable amount of~~ much time reading.

considered to be

Overdone. Use the verb *considered*.

Marlon Brando is considered ~~to be~~ one of our great actors.

considering the fact that

Trim this long phrase to the word *because*.

~~Considering the fact that~~ because mortgage rates are low, now is the time to buy.

consolidate

Flashy verb for *combine*, *join*, *merge*, or *unite*.

constant nagging

If it involves *nagging*, it must be *constant*.

Because of ~~constant~~ nagging, he became more withdrawn.

constantly evolving, constantly maintained

If things are *evolving* and *maintained*, it's probably *constant*.

English, as a language, is ~~constantly~~ evolving.

Unlike other websites, ours is ~~constantly~~ maintained.

constitutes

Big word for the simpler words *composes* or *forms*.

contains a summary of
The verb *summarizes* can replace this phrase.
The file ~~contains a summary of~~ *summarizes all the changes.*

contemplate
Big word for the simpler words *consider*, *ponder*, *reflect*, or
think.

contemporaneous in age
Word overkill. Just say *contemporaneous*.
The scholarly students were contemporaneous ~~in age~~.

contented and pleased, delighted and pleased
Redundant adjectives. Choose one or the other but not both.
We felt contented ~~and pleased~~ *over the election results.*
She was delighted ~~and pleased~~ *to co-sign on his behalf.*

contiguous to
Hefty phrase for *adjoining*, *next to*, or *touching*.

contingent
Bulky noun for *body*, *group*, or *party*.

continual and ongoing
Repetition. Choose either *continual* or *ongoing*.
Training is a continual ~~and ongoing~~ *part of our process.*

continue into the future, continue on, continue to persist, continue to remain
Continue alone is plenty for *each* phrase.
Undocumented epidemics of HIV continue ~~to persist~~.

continuously without interruption
Repetition. *Continuously* means *without interruption*.
It operates continuously ~~without interruption~~ *for eight hours.*

contract agreement, grant agreement

Overstated. Use the words *contract* or *grant*.
They approved a contract ~~agreement~~ with better healthcare.
They complied with the terms of the recent grant ~~agreement~~.

contribute

Inflated verb for *add* or *give*.

contributing factor

Redundant. *Factors* to something imply *contribution*.
Price increases are a ~~contributing~~ factor to high poverty.

controversial issue

Redundant. *Issues* are usually *controversial*.
The UN delegates began to debate the ~~controversial~~ issues.

convention (of doing things)

Big word for the simpler words *practice* or *rule*.

conventional (way)

Big word for the simpler word *usual*.

conversational dialogue

Redundant. *Dialogue* is *conversational*.
She engaged the shy student in ~~conversational~~ dialogue.

convicted felon

All *felons* are *convicted*.
Certain states prohibit ~~convicted~~ felons from voting.

core essence

Excess modifier.
We educated them with the ~~core~~ essence of our goals.

correctional facility

The words *jail* or *prison* could replace this phrase.

correspond back and forth

Redundant. *Correspondence* is always *back and forth*.
We'll correspond ~~back and forth~~ whenever it's convenient.

cost a total of, cost the sum of

Chatty. Use the verb *cost* for both phrases.
The college's renovations may cost ~~a total of~~ $20 million.

cost impact considerations

Rambling. The word *costs* can replace this noun cluster.
What cost(s) ~~impact considerations~~ are in the proposal?

costs and expenses

Redundant nouns. Either word will do.
The jury awarded her all incurred costs ~~and expenses~~.

could perhaps, could possibly, could potentially

Usually *could* by itself will do.
Our platform could ~~perhaps~~ interest some new voters.
Regular vitamins could ~~possibly~~ help one's stamina.
Forgetting the directions could ~~potentially~~ cause a problem.

could see

Weak construction. Use a stronger verb when possible.
The advisor ~~could see~~ *saw* a quick solution to the problem.

countermand

Stuffy verb for the simpler *cancel*, *recall*, or *stop*.

courageous and brave

Redundant adjectives. Choose one or the other but not both.
Unlike others, she is courageous ~~and brave~~ to try.

crisis situation, emergency situation

Redundant. Any *crisis* or *emergency* is a *situation*.
Managing a crisis ~~situation~~ takes careful planning.
If an emergency ~~situation~~ should occur, use the exit door.

crumble apart, separate them apart, split apart

Overstated. The word *apart* is not needed.
The salty sea caused the coastal levee to crumble ~~apart~~.
Once the items arrive, we will separate them ~~apart~~.
Though difficult, an atom's nucleus can be split ~~apart~~.

crystal clear

The word *crystal* is overstated.
Our cable system has ~~crystal~~ clear and static-free reception.

cumulative

Heavy word for *collective*, *growing*, or *swelling*.

current

Needless introductory word in phrases such as
current fad, *current incumbent*, *current news*, *current record*,
current status, and *current trend*.
The district's ~~current~~ incumbent is in a competitive race.

currently being, currently in progress, currently pending, currently undergoing, currently underway

The word *currently* is not needed in all these phrases.
She is ~~currently~~ being considered for the top position.
The workforce reduction notification is ~~currently~~ in progress.
He gave us a quick snapshot of what is ~~currently~~ pending.
The building is ~~currently~~ undergoing a major renovation.
The highway changes are ~~currently~~ underway in the county.

curved arc

Unessential modifier. All *arcs* are *curved*.
The blade's ~~curved~~ arc kept the wood from slipping.

cutbacks

Just use the noun *cuts*.
Amid the cuts ~~cutbacks~~, gloom reigned at the company.

D

"Simplicity is the ultimate sophistication."—Leonardo da Vinci

daily per diem
Redundant. *Per diem* implies something *daily*.

damp fog, moist fog
Overstated. All fogs are *damp* or *moist*.

dangerous hazard, dangerous lightning, dangerous weapon
Hazards, *lightning*, and *weapons* are always *dangerous*.
Carbon monoxide can easily pose a ~~dangerous~~ hazard.
Safeguarding residents from ~~dangerous~~ lightning is our goal.
Having a firearm or other ~~dangerous~~ weapon is not allowed.

dashed quickly, raced quickly
Pointless adverb. Any *dash* or *race* is done *quickly*.
Hope for a reconciliation between them was dashed ~~quickly~~.
Both attorneys raced ~~quickly~~ through their summations.

deactivate
Hefty word for *end* or *stop*.

dead and gone
Redundant. Choose one or the other but not both.
Probably their company will be ~~dead and~~ gone next year.

dead body, dead cadaver, dead corpse
Redundant. All three things imply being *dead*.
The police found the ~~dead~~ body near the interstate.

deadline date
The word *deadline* is plenty.
They extended the deadline ~~date~~ for the job applications.

deadly killer

If it's a *killer*, it must be *deadly*.
A ~~deadly~~ killer today in everyday products is aspartame.

debate about

See entry for **average about, know about**.

decade of the 60s, 70s, 80s, etc.

Verbose. Omit the phrase *decade of the*.
Our favorite songs were during the ~~decade of the~~ 60s.

deceitful lie, deceptive lie, deliberate lie

All *lies* can be *deceptive*, *deceitful*, or *deliberate*.
We prefer hearing authentic stories rather than ~~deceitful~~ lies.
It's a ~~deceptive~~ lie that he's serving his own agenda.
The statement was a ~~deliberate~~ lie by the accused.

decentralize

Large verb for the simpler verbs *divide* or *scatter*.

decide on

The ending preposition *on* is needless.
She is going to decide ~~on~~ whether to run for office.

deficiency

Big noun for the simpler noun *lack*.

defined as

This phrase is sometimes not needed.
Drugs are ~~defined as~~ substances affecting bodily functions.

definite decision

Redundant. A *decision* is something *definite*.
No ~~definite~~ decision on the proposed delay has been made.

definitely

This word can often be removed.
They ~~definitely~~ decided to support universal health care.

(the) degree to which

The phrase *how much* is simpler.
~~The degree to which~~ how much laptops cost is a concern.

deleterious

Deadly, *harmful*, or *toxic are* much simpler words.

deliberate arson, deliberate fraud, deliberate planning

Redundant. *Arson*, *fraud*, and *planning* are *deliberate*.

deliberately on purpose

The word *deliberately* is plenty.
The reporter deliberately ~~on purpose~~ asked tough questions.

delicate surgery

Redundant. All *surgery* is *delicate*.
She will undergo ~~delicate~~ surgery to remove a brain tumor.

delineate

Complex verb for *define*, *describe*, *explain*, or *outline*.

demanded insistently

Word overkill. The word *insistently* is unnecessary.
They demanded ~~insistently~~ proper steps must be taken.

demonstrate

Plush verb. Use the simpler verbs *display*, *prove*, or *show*.

depreciate in value

Needless ending phrase. The word *depreciate* is plenty by itself.
A new car depreciates ~~in value~~ the second it leaves the lot.

derived from

This phrase can often be replaced with the word *of*.
Note the benefit ~~derived from~~ of using higher octane fuel.

designate

Prefer the familiar verbs *appoint*, *name*, or *show*.

designed to

Often the ending preposition *to* can be cut.
If it works as it's designed ~~to~~, the phone will charge quickly.

desirable benefits

Redundant. *Benefits* are always *desirable*.
We have a few ~~desirable~~ benefits like medical coverage.

despite the fact that, in spite of the fact that

Pare these wordy phrases to *although*, *despite*, or *even though*.
~~Despite the fact that~~ although we lost, we all played well.
~~In spite of the fact that~~ despite not having had a hit in years, fans still flock to their concerts.

detailed information

Tired business letter prose. Use the noun *details*.
Please visit the website for more ~~detailed information~~ details.

deteriorate

Big word for the simpler words *decline*, *impair*, or *weaken*.

detrimental

The smaller words *damaging* or *harmful* can replace this big word.

dialogue (as a verb)

Lush word for *chat*, *discuss*, or *talk*.

diametrically opposed

Word overkill. The word *opposed* is fine by itself.
We confronted two ~~diametrically~~ opposed policies.

did not accept, did not allow, did not comply with, did not consider, did not pay attention to, did not remember, did not stay, did not succeed

These long phrases can be replaced with a single verb.

They ~~did not accept~~ rejected the possible buyer's final offer.

She ~~did not allow~~ prevented testimony from being heard.

He ~~did not comply with~~ violated many rules of the game.

She ~~did not consider~~ ignored what others had to say.

He ~~did not pay attention to~~ ignored all the outside noise.

He ~~did not remember~~ forgot to set his clock ahead last night.

She ~~did not stay~~ left.

She ~~did not succeed~~ failed in starting her own business.

differ from each other

Just go with the word *differ* for this phrase.

I explained how marketing and sales differ ~~from each other~~.

(a) difference of

At times, this phrase can be omitted.

The length must be reduced by ~~a difference of~~ six inches.

different and distinct

Repetition. Choose one or the other but not both.

We identified four different ~~and distinct~~ ways to help them.

different kinds, different variation, different varieties

Overstated because *different* is already implied. Omit it.

We had six ~~different~~ kinds of ice cream at the party.

We saw how ~~different~~ variation strategies can work well.

With ~~different~~ tomato varieties, taste can vary a lot.

difficult dilemma

Redundant. Any *dilemma* is *difficult*.

They face a ~~difficult~~ dilemma with their home finances.

diminutive

Adjectives like *little*, *small*, or *tiny* are simpler.

direct confrontation

Redundant. You would never have an *indirect confrontation*.
We've always tried to avoid any ~~direct~~ confrontation.

disappear from sight, disappear from view

Unneeded ending phrase. Use *disappear* alone.
At a certain distance, the dot will disappear ~~from sight~~.
The sun will soon disappear ~~from view~~ at the north pole.

disclose for the first time, divulge for the first time

Needless ending phrase. Just use *disclose* and *divulge*.
Officials are disclosing ~~for the first time~~ their salaries.
Reporters must divulge ~~for the first time~~ their sources.

discontentment

The simpler word *discontent* will do.

discontinue

Bulky word for *cease, drop, halt,* or *stop*.

discriminated against

Sometimes the word *against* is excess.
We felt the group was being discriminated ~~against~~.

disesteemed

The word *disliked* is more common and precise.

disintegrate into pieces

Excess ending phrase. The verb *disintegrate* is plenty.
As the comet fell, it started to disintegrate ~~into pieces~~.

disorganized mess

We can assume a *mess* is *disorganized*.
In no time, my desk can turn into a ~~disorganized~~ mess.

dispose of

The preposition *of* can sometimes be discarded.
She showed us how to dispose ~~of~~ the unsafe pesticides.

disseminate
Large verb for *scatter*, *send*, or *spread*.

(a) distance of
A short phrase we can often omit.
A 20 kilometer road race equals ~~a distance of~~ 12.4 miles.

distinguish between
The word *distinguish* can stand alone.
The agronomist could distinguish ~~between~~ the grass types.

divide in half
The word *halve* is plenty.
Human cells can grow bigger and then ~~divide in half~~ halve.

do a draft of
Replace this phrase with the simple verb *draft*.
My firm asked me to ~~do a~~ draft ~~of~~ a malpractice complaint.

do an inspection of
The verbs *inspect* or *check* are far less cluttered.
Do we need to ~~do an inspection of~~ inspect the new tools?

do away with
Replace this phrase with the words *end* or *stop*.
The company wants to ~~do away with~~ end telecommuting.

do not believe
Roundabout. A more direct expression would be *doubt*.
Some scientists ~~do not believe~~ doubt the powers of ESP.

doctorate degree
Redundant. A *doctorate* is a *degree*.
Dan plans on completing his doctorate ~~degree~~ in the fall.

does not have
Dense. The verb *lacks* is crisper.
My college ~~does not have~~ lacks a major in journalism.

does not have the ability to

Long-winded. A better choice is the verb *cannot*.
She ~~does not have the ability to~~ cannot access the system.

does not include

Long-winded. Use the verbs *excludes* or *omits*.
The advertised price ~~does not include~~ excludes gratuities.

does not lend itself well to

The phrase *is not fitting* is tighter.
His method ~~does not lend itself well to~~ is not fitting for the job.

does the printing

Lengthy. Use the verb *prints*.
Our new machine ~~does the printing~~ prints quickly.

done deal

Redundant. When a *deal* is *done*, it's over.
The expected company merger is not yet a ~~done~~ deal.

doomed to fail

Trim this phrase to the simple word *doomed*.
A few businesses within our city are doomed ~~to fail~~ next year.

down

The word *down* can be a needless ending preposition.
We took a 2 MB file and compressed it ~~down~~ to almost 600 KB.
After much debate, the controversial issue finally died ~~down~~.
By simplifying things ~~down~~, we'll understand the material easier.
With the sun shining ~~down~~ early, it looked to be a good day.
Write ~~down~~ the goals necessary for the class to be a success.

Other examples to consider include:

burn down	crouch down
calm down	cut down
close down	descend down
cool down	decrease down
condense down	diminish down

dive down	pour down
drill down	quiet down
drink down	reduce down
drip down	settle down
drop down	shrink down
dwindle down	shut down
fall down	sink down
falling down	sit down
hanging down	slip down
hunt down	slow down
kneel down	swallow down
melt down	swoop down
narrow down	track down
pare down	trickle down
pinpoint down	trim down
plummet down	whittle down
plunge down	winnow down

down in the basement

Redundant. You would never say *up in the basement*.
What books ~~down~~ in the store's basement did you find?

downward

At times, this word can be trimmed to *down*.
After jumping, he quickly fell down~~ward~~ like a rock.

downward descent

Redundant. *Descents* are always *downward*.
Shortly we'll begin our ~~downward~~ descent to the airport.

draft beer on tap

The phrase *on tap* is surplus.
The restaurant offered both bottled and draft beer ~~on tap~~.

draw to a close

Swap this phrase for the words *close*, *end*, *halt*, or *stop*.
After a ten-year run, the play will ~~draw to a~~ close Sunday.

draw to a conclusion

Muddle. Use the verbs *conclude*, *end*, *halt*, or *stop*.
As the trial ends ~~draws to a conclusion~~, the evidence is weak.

draw to your attention to

Wordy. The phrase *point to* is shorter.
I now ~~draw to your attention~~ point to today's guest panel.

driving force

Overstated. The word *force* by itself will do.
She has been a ~~driving~~ force in disability law for decades.

due and owing, due and payable

Repetition. Choose one or the other but not both.
The tax due ~~and owing~~ for the business was $2 million.
Penalties accruing shall be ~~due and~~ payable in 45 days.

due to the effects

At times, the word *because* can replace this phrase.
He lost hair ~~due to the effects~~ because of chemotherapy.

due to the fact that

See entry for **because of the fact that, given the fact that**.

dull thud

Sometimes *dull* is an unneeded modifier.
The much hyped film landed in theaters with a ~~dull~~ thud.

duly noted

Sometimes *duly* is an unnecessary modifier.
The witness' testimony was ~~duly~~ noted in the courtroom.

duplicate (verb)

Prefer the familiar verb *copy*.

duplicate copy

Repetition. Choose one or the other but not both.
We need to make a ~~duplicate~~ copy of the bill.

(a) duration of

Verbose. At times, this phrase can be cut.

The cell phone operated for ~~a duration of~~ two years.

during the course of, during the time that

Long-winded. Use the words *during* or *while*.

She looked calm during ~~the course of~~ the trial.

A bill passed ~~during the time that~~ while you were absent.

E

"Most editors are failed writers—but so are most writers."
—T.S. Eliot

each and every

Redundant adjectives. Choose one or the other but not both.
Each ~~and every~~ comment will be addressed immediately.

each individual

Overstated. *Each* or *everyone* can replace this phrase.
The company met the needs of each ~~individual~~ customer.
~~Each individual~~ everyone is required to have a passport.

each one

Excess. Trim this phrase to simply the word *each*.
Each ~~one~~ of us should do our best to curb greenhouse gases.

earlier in time (than)

Rambling. Sometimes you can just use the word *before*.
The Dave Clark 5 toured the U.S. before ~~earlier in time than~~ the Beatles.

early beginning, early pioneer

Redundant. *Beginning* and *pioneer* imply the word *early*.
We studied French history from its ~~early~~ beginnings until now.
Frederick Soddy was ~~an early~~ pioneer in radiochemistry.

early on

On is an unessential ending preposition.
Studies show viruses in babies may cause asthma early ~~on~~.

echelon

Hefty word for *level* or *rank*.

economically deprived, economically prohibitive

The word *poor* and the phrase *too costly* are simpler.

The ~~economically deprived~~ poor areas increased last year.

Taxes made it ~~economically prohibitive~~ too costly to live there.

edifice

The word *building* is much simpler.

effect many changes in

Dense. Try using the verb *change*.

The law will ~~effect many changes in~~ change foreign policy.

effects a reduction, effects an improvement in

Trim these phrases to simply *reduces* or *improves*.

effectuate

Large word for the simpler words *achieve*, *cause*, *do*, or *realize*.

effusive

Stuffy word for *loud*, *wordy*, or *talkative*.

either one, either one or the other

The word *either* will usually do in both cases.

The manager does not like either ~~one of the~~ options.

Either ~~one or the other of the~~ courses will be required.

ejected from the game

Rambling. Use the verb *ejected*.

The player was ejected ~~from the game~~ for misconduct.

electrical voltage

Redundant. *Electric* implies *voltage*.

The ~~electrical~~ voltage in our house can vary daily.

electronic email

Redundant. The *e* in *email* means electronic.

eliminate altogether, eliminate entirely

Verbose. Use the verbs *cut* or *end* for either phrase.
Automation may ~~eliminate altogether~~ cut many jobs.

eliminate and remove

Redundant verbs. Go with the simpler word *remove*.
The disinfectant will ~~eliminate and~~ remove all odors.

elongate

Big word for the simpler words *extend*, *lengthen*, or *stretch*.

elucidate

Elegant word for *clarify*, *explain*, *expose*, or *reveal*.

emasculate

Stuffy word. Try *reduce* or *weaken* instead.

emergency situation, crisis situation

Redundant. Any *emergency* or *crisis* is a *situation*.
If an emergency ~~situation~~ should occur, use the exit door.
Managing a crisis ~~situation~~ takes careful planning.

emolument

Big word. Try the simpler word *pay*.

emphatically stress

The word *emphatically* is surplus.
They ~~emphatically~~ stress career failure can touch many of us.

employ

Large word. Try a simpler word like *use* instead.

empty blank, empty void

The modifier *empty* is unnecessary in these phrases.
Please fill in all the ~~empty~~ blanks on the application.
His departure from the band left an ~~empty~~ void.

emulate
Complex word for *copy*, *follow*, or *imitate*.

enables you to
Tighten the writing by using the phrase *lets you*.
The software lets ~~enables~~ you ~~to~~ add new data automatically.

enclosed for your information, enclosed herein, enclosed herewith, enclosed with this letter
The word *enclosed* can usually replace these tired phrases.
Enclosed ~~for your information~~ is the data you requested.

enclosed in parentheses
The verb *enclosed* is excess here.
Usually the local area code is ~~enclosed~~ in parentheses.

end of year annual report
Redundant. *Annual report* comes at the *end of the year*.
The ~~end-of-year~~ annual report will be mailed next week.

end result
Unneeded modifier. The noun *result* is all you need.
The ~~end~~ result was lower prices and better service.

endeavor
Try is a much simpler verb.

ended the talk with
Chatty. Try using just the verb *ended*.
He ~~ended the talk with~~ ended with a short slide show.

endemically widespread
The word *endemically* can often be discarded.
The virus outbreak appears ~~endemically~~ widespread.

ending outcome
Redundant. *Outcomes* are always at the *end*.
Because of tape delay, I knew the game's ~~ending~~ outcome.

enervate

The word *weaken* is a simpler word choice.

engage in conversations

Time waster. The word *talk* will do.
We do ~~engage in conversations~~ talk with our customers.

enter into a contract, enter into an agreement

Formal wordy phrase for *agree* or *contract*.
We authorized the city to ~~enter into a~~ contract with the firm.
We ~~entered into an agreement~~ agreed to a two-year lease.

enter a bid

Windy. The verb *bid* is simpler.
No one will be permitted to ~~enter a~~ bid until 9 a.m.

entire monopoly

Overstated. Use the word *monopoly* by itself.
They want ~~an entire~~ monopoly of the software business.

entirely complete, entirely eliminate

Often these qualifiers can be deleted.
Next week the research project will be ~~entirely~~ complete.
We ~~entirely~~ eliminated all the hardware problems.

enumerate

Try simpler verbs such as *count*, *list*, *name*, or *number*.

enunciate

Words like *pronounce*, *speak*, or *utter* are less inflated.

envisage

Big word for the simpler words *expect*, *imagine*, *picture*, or *see*.

ephemeral

Brief, fleeting, or *passing* are simpler word choices.

equal to one another

Overdone. The word *equal* by itself will do.

Base angles in an isosceles triangle are equal ~~to one another~~.

equally as

Surplus. The word *equally* is typically not needed.

Experience can be ~~equally~~ as valuable as one's education.

equipped with

The words *has* or *have* are more concise choices.

What rooms ~~are equipped with~~ have videoconferencing?

equitable

Bloated word for *fair* or *just*.

equivalent

The word *equal* or the phrase *the same* are simpler options.

eradicate

The word *destroy* is a much simpler synonym; however, if you do use *eradicate*, it should stand alone and *never be qualified* by another word.

Examples where it's incorrectly qualified include:

completely eradicate	totally eradicate
fully eradicate	utterly eradicate
thoroughly eradicate	wholly eradicate

erroneous

Hollow word for *incorrect* or *wrong*.

erroneous error

Word overkill. The word *error* by itself will do.

The PC command gave me an ~~erroneous~~ error message.

eschew

Legalistic jargon. Try the phrase *give up* instead.

essential condition, essential core, essential necessity, essential prerequisite

The word *essential* is a needless modifier.
Her theory was based on one ~~essential~~ condition.
His paper discussed the ~~essential~~ core values of living.
Access to data is ~~an essential~~ necessity for the workers.
Empowerment is ~~an essential~~ prerequisite of leadership.

essentially

Weighty word that seldom adds anything and often can be cut.
Mankind has existed ~~essentially~~ unchanged for years.

establish

Simpler verbs are *launch*, *set*, or *start.*

establish conclusive evidence

The word *prove* can replace this phrase.
He must ~~establish conclusive evidence~~ prove she acted alone.

established

Overworked and uncalled-for introductory word.
They abandoned ~~an established~~ tradition of holiday travel.

Other possibilities to consider include:

established custom	established protocol
established fact	established record
established norm	established standard
established precedent	

(an) estimated

About, *almost*, *around*, *nearly*, or *roughly* are crisper words.
~~An estimated~~ almost 5,000 people attended the celebration.

estimated at (about, almost, around, nearly, roughly)

This phrase should not include any of the parenthetical words above.
The percentage of failing grades is estimated at ~~about~~ 20.

Note: You could also omit the phrase *estimated at* and use any of the five parenthetical words alone.
The percentage of failing grades is ~~estimated at~~ about 20.

evanescent

Bloated word. *Brief*, *fleeting*, or *passing* are simpler words.

even balance

Overstated. Use *balance* alone.
We have ~~an even~~ a balance of male and female soloists.

even though

Overdone. The word *although* is shorter.

evening soiree, evening sunset

Redundant. Both *soirees* and *sunsets* are in the evening.
We attended an ~~evening~~ soiree and wine-tasting event.
Last year we took a ~~evening~~ sunset cruise on Lake George.

eventually in the future, eventually inevitable, eventually later

Wordy phrases that can be reduced.
Eventually ~~in the future~~ we will solve the energy problem.
Do not delay the ~~eventually~~ inevitable problem we face.
They ~~eventually~~ later discussed the new city budget.

ever

The word *ever* is sometimes not needed. Examples include:
The school posted its best ~~ever~~ SAT scores this year.
The biggest ~~ever~~ budget surplus cut the debt in half.
The company posted its first ~~ever~~ quarterly profit.
She would never ~~ever~~ change her political affiliation.
We seldom ~~ever~~ fail to achieve our business objectives.

ever before

Word overkill. The word *before* is not needed.
More taxpayers are using electronic filing than ever ~~before~~.

everlasting eternity

Redundant. *Eternity* means *everlasting*.
An ~~everlasting~~ eternity of peace awaits those of that faith.

every day, every month, every week, every year

Fatty phrases. The words *daily*, *monthly*, *weekly*, and *yearly* are leaner.
He tries to balance his checkbook ~~every month~~ monthly.

every effort will be made

Trite business phrase that can be reduced to *we'll try*.
~~Every effort will be made~~ we'll try to refund the full amount.

every individual one

Excess. The word *one* is not needed.
We believe every individual ~~one~~ needs a chance to succeed.

every now and then

Talkative. Go with the word *occasionally* instead.
~~Every now and then~~ occasionally we take a look at our investments.

every single

Overstated. Delete the word *single*.
We cannot fairly evaluate every ~~single~~ candidate.

evolve over time

Redundant. It's assumed *evolving* is over *time*.
Software evolves ~~over time~~ with new features in each release.

exact

Uncalled-for introductory word.
Although they are ~~exact~~ opposites, they get along well.

Other examples to consider include:

exact counterpart
exact duplicate
exact equal
exact equivalent
exact identical

exact match
exact mirror image
exact replica
exact same

exact and precise

Repetition. Choose one or the other but not both.
Unlike writing, math is an exact ~~and precise~~ subject.

exactly alike, exactly correct, exactly identical, exactly right, exactly sure, exactly the same

The word *exactly* is surplus in each phrase.
No two snowflakes or twins are ~~exactly~~ alike.
You're ~~exactly~~ correct in thinking fish oil is healthful.
His estimate is ~~exactly~~ identical to the other contractor.
Some think your mathematical theory is ~~exactly~~ right.
We're not ~~exactly~~ sure of the filename he gave the report.
As we've heard, no two fingerprints are ~~exactly~~ the same.

(an) example of this

The phrase *for example* is a better choice.

except in a small number of cases

Clutter. Use the word *usually*.
~~Except in a small number of cases~~ usually the antibiotic works.

except when

Roundabout. *Unless* is more direct.
He hates regulation ~~except when~~ unless it suits him politically.

excess verbiage, excess waste

Redundant. *Verbiage* and *waste* are always to an *excess*.
~~Excess~~ verbiage can be a destroyer of message clarity.
The company vows to treat the ~~excess~~ liquid waste soon.

(an) excessive number of

Verbose. *Too many* is a crisper phrase.
The college has ~~an excessive number of~~ too many applicants.

excruciatingly painful

Redundant. Something *excruciating* is *painful*.
It's been excruciating~~ly painful~~ to see the team's demise.

exemplary
Ideal, excellent, or *outstanding* are simpler word choices.

exercises control over
Muddle. Use the verb *controls*.
She ~~exercises control over~~ controls all subcontracting here.

exhaustive
Bulky word for *complete*, *full*, or *thorough*.

exhibit a tendency to, exhibit improvement
Overload. The phrase *tend to* or the verb *improve* is plenty.
The plants ~~exhibit a tendency~~ tend to grow toward sunlight.
The plants ~~exhibit improvement~~ improve with more sunlight.

exhibits the ability to
Tedious. The simple word *can* could replace this phrase.
That employee ~~exhibits the ability to~~ can handle many tasks.

existing
Unnecessary. Often this word can be removed.
The report recaps the ~~existing~~ Wall Street conditions.

existing loan, outstanding loan
Overdone. All loans are either *existing* or *outstanding*.
Refinancing your ~~existing~~ loan will result in a higher rate.
For once, they do not have any ~~outstanding~~ car loans.

exonerate
Inflated word for *acquit*, *clear*, *pardon*, or *relieve*.

expedite
The words *hasten*, *hurry*, or *rush* are simpler word choices.

expeditious
Stuffy word for *fast*, *prompt*, *quick,* or *swift*.

expend
The words *pay* or *spend* are simpler options.

expenditure
Lengthy word. *Charge*, *cost*, *expense,* or *spend* are shorter.

expenses and costs
Redundant nouns. Either word will do.
The jury awarded her all incurred expenses ~~and costs~~.

experiencing personally
Redundant. If you *experience* something, it is *personal*.
We must decide if it's all worth experiencing ~~personally~~.

explain and justify
Redundant verbs. Choose one or the other but not both.
The auditor failed to ~~explain and~~ justify the cost overruns.

explicit
Large word. *Clear*, *open*, or *plain* are simpler word choices.

exposed opening
Needless modifier. Use the word *opening* by itself.
The vent lets cold air enter through an ~~exposed~~ opening.

express opposition to, express regret, express skepticism about, express sorrow
Fatty phrases. The words *oppose*, *regret*, *question*, and *grieve* are leaner.
The council did ~~express opposition to~~ oppose the budget.
She and others ~~express~~ regret their votes for the war.
We ~~expressed skepticism about~~ questioned the stimulus plan.
They ~~expressed sorrow~~ grieved over their sudden loss.

extend an invitation to
Roundabout. The word *invite* is more direct.
We would like to ~~extend an invitation to~~ invite you next week.

extensively throughout

The word *extensively* is surplus in this phrase.
In her youth, she traveled ~~extensively~~ throughout the U.S.

(the) extent of

At times, this whole phrase can be omitted.
~~The extent of~~ their teaching experience is impressive.

extra added bonus, extra added feature,
extra added special

Overload. The word *extra* alone will do in each case.
As an extra ~~added bonus~~, you can have next Friday off.

extravagant

Hefty word for *costly* or *wasteful*.

extreme in degree

Inflated. The descriptive word *extreme* is plenty.
Their conduct was outrageous and extreme ~~in degree~~.

extremity

The words *edge*, *end*, or *limit* are simpler words.

F

"You don't write because you want to say something, you write because you have something to say."—F. Scott Fitzgerald

fabricate
Complex verb. Prefer the simpler verbs *build* or *make*.

face mask
Sometimes the word *face* is not needed.
To protect my fractured cheekbone, I wore a ~~face~~ mask.

face-to-face confrontation
Redundant. *Confrontations* are *face to face*.
She avoided the humiliation of a ~~face-to-face~~ confrontation.

face up to
Wordy. This phrase can typically be shortened.
Without hesitation, we should face ~~up to~~ our mistakes.

facilitate
Grandiose. Use the words *aid*, *ease*, or *help*.

(the) fact of the matter is, (the) fact that
Long-winded. Often these phrases can be shortened.
The fact ~~of the matter~~ is we made a simple mistake.
We accept ~~the fact that~~ some things are not meant to be.

factual and accurate
Verbal surplus. One of these words will do.
The diagrams in the book are factual ~~and accurate~~.

factual basis
Fatty phrase. This can be trimmed to the words *fact*, *reason*, or *truth*.
The statement provides a ~~factual basis~~ reason for the plea.

fail to comply with

Clutter. The words *defy*, *disobey*, or *violate* can replace this phrase.

If you ~~fail to comply with~~ defy the law, penalties will occur.

fair and equitable, fair and just, fair and square

Overstated. Simply say *fair*, *just*, or *fairly*.

We provide fair ~~and equitable~~ treatment to all workers.
The company gives ~~fair and~~ just wages for all employees.
The votes show the candidate won fairly ~~fair and square~~.

fairytale story

Redundant. A *fairytale* is a *story*.

Today the teacher read a fairytale ~~story~~ to her students.

the fall season

Overstated. It's implied *fall* is a *season*.

Our leaves turn colors early in ~~the~~ fall ~~season~~.

false

At times, this word is a needless modifier.

Her doctor feels sunscreens create ~~false~~ illusions of safety.

Other possibilities to consider include:

false fabrication	false front
false facade	false misrepresentation
false fallacy	false pretense

false and misleading

Repetition. Use *false* or *misleading* but not both.

He gave ~~false and~~ misleading testimony during the hearing.

falsely padded

Word overkill. Omit the word *falsely*.

Some workers ~~falsely~~ padded their expense accounts.

familiar friend

Redundant. Every *friend* must be *familiar*.
Bob is more a ~~familiar~~ friend than a mere acquaintance.

far and wide

The words *broadly* or *widely* are simpler one-word choices.
Her influence was felt ~~far and wide~~ widely throughout the state.

far away from

Overdone. The word *away* is not always needed.
The new houses were kept far ~~away~~ from the nuclear plant.

For more examples, see entry for the word **away**.

farewell swan song, final swan song, last swan song

Redundant modifiers. *Swan song* means something that's ending.
"Utopia" was Laurel and Hardy's ~~farewell~~ swan song film.

fastest ever

Excess. The word *fastest* by itself is enough.
Next year the company will build its fastest computer ~~ever~~.

fatal drowning, fatal suicide

Redundant. *Drowning* and *suicides* are always fatal.
The paper reported a ~~fatal~~ drowning last week.
Firearms is a common ~~fatal~~ suicide method used by some.

favorable approval

Redundant. An *approval* is something *favorable*.
Her ~~favorable~~ approval rating is rising each month.

favored to win

Unneeded ending phrase.
Even before the odds are set, the team is favored ~~to win~~.

feature

Sometimes this word can be dropped.
The alarm clock has a built-in delay ~~feature~~.

feel inside

Word overkill. Use the verb *feel* alone.
Few people know how I feel ~~inside~~ about the decision.

fellow classmate, fellow colleague, fellow comrade, fellow co-worker, fellow peer, fellow teammate

The word *fellow* is a pointless modifier in each phrase.
We enjoyed the 20th reunion with our ~~fellow~~ classmates.

ferry boat

Word overkill. Use the word *ferry* by itself.
For years we took the ferry ~~boat~~ across the Hudson river.

few and far between

Filler phrase. Words like rare, scarce, or sparse can replace this phrase.
High salary raises are ~~few and far between~~ rare today.

few in number

Extra words. The word *few* alone will do.
Are the votes too few ~~in number~~ to make a difference?

fictional novel

Redundant. Every *novel* is *fictional*.
"The Firm" is a popular ~~fictional~~ novel by John Grisham.

(the) field of

This phrase is usually surplus.
She is majoring in ~~the field of~~ math and physics.

fierce battle, violent battle

Redundant. Battles are typically *fierce* or *violent*.
Congress waged a ~~fierce~~ battle over the latest spending bill.

fiery conflagration

Excess modifier.
The ~~fiery~~ conflagration surged toward the neighborhoods.

file an application, submit an application

Rambling. Use the verb *apply*.
To be safe, you need to ~~file an application~~ apply now.
Did you ~~submit an application~~ apply for the job?

fill to capacity, fill to the brim

Excess ending phrases.
This year's expo is filled ~~to capacity~~ with exhibitors.
When we fill it ~~to the brim~~, the cup holds 12 ounces.

filthy dirty

Overstated. Pick either *filthy* or *dirty*.
The forest fire's fallout ash made everything ~~filthy~~ dirty.

final

A much overused and implied modifier.
The construction was nearing ~~final~~ completion.
What was the ~~final~~ outcome of the negotiations?

Other examples where the word *final* is unnecessary:

final adieu	final ending
final climax	final farewell
final conclusion	final resolution
final culmination	final result
final demise	final settlement
final destination	final showdown
final end	final upshot

final and irrevocable

To avoid this redundancy, stay with the word *final*.
The decision to overturn the verdict is final ~~and irrevocable~~.

finalization

Overblown. Use the noun *end.*

finalize

Plush verb for *decide*, *end*, *finish*, or *settle*.

finally ended, finally settled

Word overkill. The word *finally* is not needed.
The search for a news anchor ~~finally~~ ended last week.
The feud between the two companies is ~~finally~~ settled.

financial resources, financial wherewithal

Posh phrases. Words like *assets*, *capital*, *cash*, *funds*, or *money* are simpler.

find out

Padding. Just say *learn*.
To ~~find out~~ learn more, select one of the following links.

fine mist

Redundant. A *mist* is always *fine*.
The humidifier's ~~fine~~ mist helped the baby's sore throat.

fire hydrant, water hydrant

Redundant. *Hydrants* pertain to *fire* or *water*.
Illegally using a ~~water~~ hydrant may jeopardize fire fighting.

firm commitment, firm conviction, firm resolution

Overdone. These things are assumed to be *firm*.
We have a ~~firm~~ commitment to our allies around the world.
If elected, he has a ~~firm~~ conviction to change the tax laws.
They made a ~~firm~~ resolution to quit smoking next year.

first

A much overused and unnecessary modifier.
We were teenagers when the league ~~first~~ began.
What year were Walkmans ~~first~~ introduced?
Some areas were ~~first~~ initially off limits.

Other possibilities to consider include:

first beginnings
first coined
first conceived
first created
first debuted
first discovered
first established
first ever
first founded

first invented
first originated
first priority
first prototype
first revealed
first started
first-time beginner
first uncovered
first unveiled

first and foremost

Verbal excess. One of these words will do.
Our concern for the needy is first and foremost.

first come into being

Long-winded. Try the words *arise*, *begin*, or *start*.
When did paper money first come into being start?

first of all, first off

Overload. Go with the word *first* for either phrase.
First of all, please welcome our new members tonight.

first time ever

Unneeded ending word.
The market passed the 13,000 mark for the first time ever.

first-time precedent

Overstated. The phrase first-time is unneeded.
Some banks set a first-time precedent for student loans.

fiscal downturn

Inflated term for the word *recession*.

flatly refused, flatly rejected

Excess modifier in both phrases.
The candidate flatly refused the company's first job offer.
Without hesitation, they flatly rejected the group's first idea.

flee quickly

Redundant. If you're *fleeing*, you're doing it *quickly*.
Because of the fire and winds, residents had to flee ~~quickly~~.

fleeting instant, fleeting moment

Redundant. *Instants* and *moments* are always *fleeting*.
For a ~~fleeting~~ moment, we were optimistic on the outcome.

floral bouquet

Overkill. Use the word *bouquet* by itself.
A ~~floral~~ bouquet of tiger lilies arrived at our house yesterday.

floundering around

Excess. The word *around* is not needed.
He was floundering ~~around~~ helplessly looking for his wallet.

flower boutonniere

Redundant. *Boutonnieres* are *flowers*.
~~Flower~~ boutonnieres require more care than regular flowers.

fly through the air

Filler phrase. The word *fly* is plenty.
Our class is studying how a bird can fly ~~through the air~~.

focal point, focus of attention

Chatty. The word *focus* by itself will do.
Lower taxes is the campaign's ~~focal point~~ focus.
Her focus ~~of attention~~ affects her learning methods.

focus in

Drawn out. Sometimes the preposition *in* is unnecessary.
We're trying to focus ~~in~~ on the real cause of the accident.

follow after, follow below

Repetition. The verb *follow* is fine by itself.
We tried to follow ~~after~~ the band to get backstage but failed.
The year's most popular stories follow ~~below~~.

follow along the lines of

Long-winded. Words like *imitate*, *match*, or *resemble* are crisper.
My offer will follow along the lines of *match your company's*.

follow behind, lag behind, leave behind, trail behind

Extra word. The word *behind* can usually be discarded.
Considering you know the way, I'll follow behind *you*.
Some students still lag behind *other countries in science*.
What did you leave behind *at the restaurant?*
Many salaries trail behind *this year's inflation rate*.

for a period of

Padded. Pare this phrase to simply the word *for*.
We will be away from the office for a period of *10 days*.

for a short space of time

Clutter. Use the phrase *for a short time*.
He'll stay and sign autographs for a short space of *time*.

for all intents and purposes

Prune this padded phrase from your communication.
For all intents and purposes *they made the difference*.

for free

Excess. Typically the word *free* is plenty.
We received some expert stock and market tips for *free*.

for purposes of

Fatty phrase. The word *for* is leaner.
The donations are for purposes of *helping the flood victims*.

for the duration of, over the duration of

Verbose. Say *during*, *throughout*, or *while*.
Her car was used for the duration of *during the TV show*.

for the express purpose of

Muddle. The word *to* is more concise.
It was done for the express purpose of *to help the animals*.

for the most part
The words *typically* or *usually* can often replace this stale phrase.
Despite differences, the teams ~~for the most~~ usually get along.

for the price of
Wordy. Use the preposition *for*.
We bought the new car for ~~the price of~~ $25,000.

for the reason that, for the simple reason, for this reason
Empty phrases. Replace with *because* or *why*.
I'm not attending ~~for the simple reason~~ because I prefer not.

for the sum of
Long-winded. Use the preposition *for*.
For ~~the sum of~~ $50, we bought five sweepstakes tickets.

for the time being
Fatty phrase. The phrase *for now* is shorter.
For ~~the time being~~ now, the enrollment stands at 20 people.

for your convenience, for your information, for your perusal
Stale business letter phrases that add little.
~~For your convenience~~ airport shuttles leave every hour.

forbearance
Big word. The simpler words *patience* or *restraint* carry the same meaning.

forecast ahead, project ahead
Repetition. The word *ahead* is surplus in both phrases.
He tried to forecast ~~ahead~~ the company's year-end revenue.
The music company will project ~~ahead~~ this year's releases.

foreign imports
Redundant. All *imports* are *foreign*.
~~Foreign~~ imports continue to gain a substantial market share.

foreign-born immigrant

Redundant. *Immigrants* are all *foreign born*.

~~Foreign-born~~ *immigrants have many of the same rights.*

forever and ever

Verbal surplus. Delete the phrase, *and ever*.

Let's make the good times last forever ~~and ever~~.

former graduate, former veteran

Redundant. *Graduate* and *veteran* imply something *former*.

Tim is a ~~former~~ graduate of the State College at Oneonta.

The ~~former~~ injured veteran was honored with a Bronze Star.

formulate

Showy word. Try the simpler verbs *devise*, *form*, *make*, or *plan*.

forthwith

Weighty word for *at once* or *now*.

fortitude

Courage, *grit*, or *strength* are simpler word choices.

fortuitous

Large word for the simpler words *accidental*, *chance*, or *lucky*.

fortunate luck

Redundant. *Luck* is assumed to be *fortunate*.

We have the ~~fortunate~~ luck of being born in this country.

forward planning, forward progress

Redundant modifiers.

Our aggressive ~~forward~~ planning benefited our retirement.

Our hospital continues to make ~~forward~~ progress on disease.

foul odor, unpleasant odor

Unneeded modifier. *Odors* are *foul* and *unpleasant*.

If you smell a(n) ~~foul~~ odor, immediately open a window.

An ~~unpleasant~~ odor continues to come from the landfill.

foundered and sank

Redundant verbs. Use *foundered* or *sank* but not both.
The Andrea Doria ~~foundered and~~ sank 11 hours after colliding.

framework

Overused word. Try *frame* or *model*.

frank candor

Redundant. *Candor* means being *frank*.
The film is rated PG for its ~~frank~~ candor and situations.

fraudulent

Inflated word for *fake*, *false*, or *sham*.

free and clear, free and gratis

Repetition. Simply go with the word *free*.
In five years, we'll be free ~~and clear~~ of the mortgage.

free and gratis, free at no cost, free gift, free giveaway, free of charge, free pass

Redundant. It's understood these things have no cost.
The children won ~~free~~ passes to the amusement park.

freezing ice

Redundant. All *ice* is *freezing*.
Last week, the entire state endured the ~~freezing~~ ice storms.

frequently

Inflated word for *often*.

friend of mine

Excess ending phrase.
A friend ~~of mine~~ has decided to pursue her law degree.

frightening scare

Redundant. All *scares* are *frightening*.
To our surprise, the film contains a few ~~frightening~~ scares.

from

The preposition *from* is sometimes not needed.

The menu had many specials that we could choose ~~from~~.

Where did you get your inspiration ~~from~~?

Many young children suffer ~~from~~ migraine headaches.

Where does the radio broadcast originate ~~from~~?

from each other

Wordy. Try deleting this phrase.

The laptops differ ~~from each other~~ in their memory capacity.

from the commercial standpoint

Talkative. Say *commercially*.

The film is a hit ~~from the commercial standpoint~~ commercially.

frown on the face

Redundant. *Faces* have *frowns*.

The colorful portrait was marked by a frown ~~on the face~~.

frozen ice, frozen tundra

Redundant. If it's *ice* or *tundra*, both are *frozen*.

Their company manufactures ~~frozen~~ ice cream novelties.

They spent two months exploring the Alaskan ~~frozen~~ tundra.

full and complete

See entry for **complete and full, complete and utter**.

full capacity, full potential, full satisfaction, full stop

The word *full* is surplus in these phrases.

The voucher program has reached ~~full~~ capacity again.

Her career with them has not reached its ~~full~~ potential.

The store prides itself on a customer's ~~full~~ satisfaction.

Remain in your seats until the aircraft comes to a ~~full~~ stop.

fully cognizant of

The phrase *aware of* is more concise.

The mayor was ~~fully cognizant~~ aware of the city's problems.

fully comprehensive, fully destroyed

Excess. The word *fully* is not needed.
They offer a ~~fully~~ comprehensive security system for houses.
As the aerial photo shows, the facility was ~~fully~~ destroyed.

functional

Overblown word for *works*.

functionality

Complex word for the much simpler *function*.

fundamental

Overblown word for *basic*.

fundamental basis, fundamental principle

Overdone. The word *fundamental* is not needed.
Physics provides the ~~fundamental~~ basis for many sciences.
To have wealth, one must master this ~~fundamental~~ principle.

furnish a solution for, furnish an explanation for

Uncover the smothered verbs *solve* and *explain*.
The report didn't ~~furnish a solution~~ solve ~~for~~ the flooding.
He should ~~furnish an explanation~~ explain ~~for~~ his absence.

further to

At times, the word *further* can be removed.
The minimum wage is being raised ~~further~~ to help others.

further to your recent communication

Stale business phrase.
Prefer: *Thank you for contacting us*.

furthermore

Bulky word for *also*, *besides*, or *more*.

future

Much overused implied modifier. Delete it.

The graduation class discussed its ~~future~~ plans.

Other possibilities to consider include:

future ahead	future potential
future development	future projection
future expectation	future prospect
future hope	future recurrence

G

"Every author in some way portrays himself in his works, even if it be against his will."—Goethe

gain entry into
Long phrase for *enter*.
We showed our badges to ~~gain entry into~~ *enter the building.*

garrulous
Stuffy word for *chatty*, *talkative*, or *wordy*.

gave an approval for, gave an explanation for
Rambling phrases for *approved* or *explained*.
The board ~~gave an approval for~~ *approved the city budget.*
He ~~gave an explanation for~~ *explained the mishap thoroughly.*

general
Uncalled-for introductory word.
Do not draw a ~~general~~ *conclusion until we know the facts.*
For some reason, they refused to sell to the ~~general~~ *public.*

Other examples to consider include:

general consensus
general custom
general facts
general pattern
general vicinity

genetic clone, genetic mutant
Nonessential modifiers. Delete the word *genetic*.
Her group does ~~genetic~~ *clone experiments on animals.*
Its odd appearance certainly suggests a ~~genetic~~ *mutant.*

genuine original, genuine sincerity
Redundant. *Original* and *sincerity* have to be *genuine*.
We bought a(n) ~~genuine~~ *original hand-embroidered blanket.*
She played the difficult role with such ~~genuine~~ *sincerity.*

genuinely real
Unneeded modifier. The word *real* alone is plenty.
The painting captured images that looked ~~genuinely~~ real.

get across
Lengthy. The words *convey* or *explain* are briefer.
He spent hours trying to ~~get across~~ explain his new theory.

get in touch with
Windy. *Call*, *contact*, *phone*, *reach*, or *write* are crisper.
Be sure to ~~get in touch with~~ contact your local representative.

get married
Just say *marry*.
We plan to ~~get married~~ marry next year.

get on the same page
Typical industry jargon that loses its impact through overuse.
Try using the phrase, *share the same thoughts*.

give a justification for, give an answer, give an apology, give an indication of
Tedious. The verbs *justify*, *answer*, *apologize*, and *show* are more compact.
She could not ~~give a justification for~~ justify her original vote.
You will be expected to ~~give an~~ answer by Monday.
No need to ~~give an apology~~ apologize; we all make mistakes.
The criteria ~~give an indication of~~ show key parts of the plan.

give and take
The word *compromise* could replace this cliché.
A serious ~~give and take~~ compromise benefits both countries.

give assistance to
Bulky. The verb *help* is a better choice.
The literacy program ~~gives assistance to~~ helps many people.

give consideration to
Muddle. Use the verb *consider*.
~~Give consideration to~~ *consider all options in our proposal*.

give due recognition to
Roundabout. The verb *recognize* is more direct.
Ensure you ~~give due recognition to~~ *recognize the entire team*.

give encouragement to
Overblown. The verb *encourage* is much shorter.
We will ~~give encouragement to~~ *encourage the team always*.

give instructions to
Verbose. Use the verb *instruct*.
The officer will ~~give instructions to~~ *instruct the new recruits*.

give offense to
Lengthy. The word *offend* is simpler.
Her speech didn't ~~give offense to~~ *offend anyone in the class*.

give proof of
Wordy. The word *prove* is tighter.
You will be asked to ~~give proof of~~ *prove your compliance*.

give rise to
Tedious. Say *cause* or *lead to*.
Too much caffeine can ~~give rise to~~ *cause hypertension*.

given
Extra word. Sometimes this word can be cut.
Only one DVR machine can operate at a ~~given~~ *time*.

given away for nothing
Needless repeating of the same idea.
Many MP3 players were given away ~~for nothing~~.

given the fact that

See entry for **because of the fact that, due to the fact that**.

glowing ember

Redundant. All *embers glow*.
We stayed by the fire until the last ~~glowing~~ ember faded.

go along with

Wordy. Verbs like *endorse*, *favor*, or *support* can replace this phrase.
I'm unsure if I can ~~go along with~~ support this latest proposal.

go get

Overkill. The word *go* can usually be deleted.
We'll ~~go~~ get a second estimate before using their services.

go on with

Long-winded. The word *continue* is more concise.
Adapt to your setbacks and ~~go on with~~ continue your life.

goals and objectives

Verbal surplus. One of these words will do.
The marketing plan mirrors the team's goals ~~and objectives~~.

goes to show

Excess words. Say *proves*, *reveals*, *shows*, etc.
It ~~goes to show~~ shows that some vitamins have risks.

graceful in appearance

Chatty. Say *graceful*.
As a dancer, Gene Kelley was graceful ~~in appearance~~.

grand slam home run

Redundant. A *grand slam* in baseball is always a *home run*.
In the top of the 9th inning, he hit a grand slam ~~home run~~.

grandiloquent

Lush word. The words *pompous* or *verbose* are simpler.

grant agreement, contract agreement

Overstated. Use the words *grant* or *contract* instead.
They complied with the terms of the recent grant ~~agreement~~.
They approved a contract ~~agreement~~ with better healthcare.

grateful thanks

Unneeded modifier. Cut the word *grateful*.
A ~~grateful~~ thanks goes to the volunteers and supporters.

grave crisis

Redundant. We can assume every *crisis* is *grave*.
In the wake of the charges, they faced a ~~grave~~ crisis.

(a) great deal of, (a) great length of

Long-winded. Use the word *much* instead.
During the surgery, she felt ~~a great deal of~~ much discomfort.
We spent ~~a great length of~~ much time advising them.

great majority

Excess modifier. Omit the word *great*.
The environment causes the ~~great~~ majority of diseases.

(a) great number of times

Tedious. The word *often* is simpler.
We used to play their records ~~a great number of times~~ often.

greater measure of, greater number of

Rambling. The word *more* is simpler.
I need to gain ~~a greater measure of~~ more confidence speaking.
I threw ~~a greater number of~~ more pitches in last night's game.

greatest percent

Overdone. The word *most* is a better choice.
Florida had the ~~greatest percent~~ most in population change.

growing greater

Unessential ending modifier. *Growing* by itself is fine.

Income distribution within the country is growing ~~greater~~.

H

"My aim is to put down on paper what I see and what I feel in the best and simplest way."—Ernest Hemingway

habitual addiction, habitual custom

Overstated. The word *habitual* is excess.
Hypnotism cured his ~~habitual~~ addiction to smoking.
Tipping 20% here seems to be the ~~habitual~~ custom.

had a consideration for

Long-winded. Pare this phrase to simply *considered*.
They ~~had a consideration for~~ considered promoting him.

had an effect upon

Clutter. The words *influenced* or *swayed* are better choices.
Her advice ~~had an effect upon~~ swayed his college choices.

had an occasion to be

Verbose. The word *was* is a shorter substitute.
He usually ~~had an occasion to be~~ was lucky.

had done before, had done previously

Overkill. *Before* and *previously* are unneeded ending words.
They did something that no other company had done ~~before~~.
They regretted everything they had done ~~previously~~.

hailing outside, raining outside, snowing outside

Redundant. *Hailing*, *raining*, and *snowing* occur *outside*.
We were surprised to see it hailing ~~outside~~ this time of year.
If it's raining ~~outside~~ tonight, the concert will be cancelled.
For the first time this winter, it's snowing ~~outside~~.

handsome looking

Needless ending word.
The book is packaged in a handsome ~~looking~~ hard cover.

hands-on experience

Redundant. *Experience* implies something being done *hands-on*.
He did the internship to get more ~~hands-on~~ experience.

happens to be

Talkative. The simple word *is* can replace this phrase.
She ~~happens to be~~ is a graduate of Vassar College.

harmful injury

Redundant. Any *injury* is *harmful*.
Stretching before exercising helps prevent ~~harmful~~ injuries.

has a considerable impact on

Lengthy. The phrase *considerably impacts* is simpler.
My design ~~has a considerable impact~~ considerably impacts it.

has a need for

Muddle. Use the verb *need*.
The company ~~has a need for~~ needs many engineers.

has a tendency to

Wasteful. Use the phrase *tends to*.
He ~~has a tendency to~~ tends to help the less fortunate often.

has an objection

Talkative. Use the verb *objects*.
The attorney ~~has an objection~~ objects to the new evidence.

has been

A touch wordy. The verb *was* is sometimes a better choice.
If you don't know, tonight's meeting ~~has been~~ was cancelled.

has been completed

Chatty. The phrase *is done* is shorter.
The project's first phase ~~has been completed~~ is done.

has proved to be, has occasion to be

Rambling. The simple verb *is* can replace these phrases.
She ~~has proved to be~~ is a valuable team player.
He ~~has occasion to be~~ is overlooked at times.

has the ability to, has the capacity to, has the opportunity to

Long-winded. Use the verb *can* for all these phrases.
She ~~has the ability to~~ can win every swimming race.
An ultra violet ray ~~has the capacity to~~ can hurt your skin.
The town ~~has the opportunity to~~ can adopt new regulations.

has the appearance of

Lengthy. The verb *appears* is simpler.
The tooth ~~has the appearance of~~ appears to be cracked.

has to do with

Verbose. Use the phrase *deals with*.
The film ~~has to do~~ deals with the history of NASCAR.

have a meeting with

Drawn out. Use the phrase *meet with*.
I must ~~have a meeting with~~ meet with him on this issue.

have a negative impact

Overstated. The words *harm* or *hurt* are more concise.
The budget cuts will ~~have a negative impact~~ hurt schools.

have a suspicion of

Tedious way to say *suspect*.
The police ~~have a suspicion of~~ suspect foul play being involved.

have and hold

Redundant verbs. Choose one or the other but not both.
That's a good stock to have ~~and hold~~ in your portfolio.

have been found to be

Wordy. Replace with the phrase *can be*.
Avocadoes ~~have been found to~~ can be helpful in lowering cholesterol.

have been shown to be

Tedious. The verb *are* is much shorter.

The vitamins ~~have been shown to be~~ *are quite effective.*

have got to

Roundabout. The word *must* is more direct.

We ~~have got to~~ *must get other students to hear his advice.*

have knowledge of

Uncover the smothered verb *know* to be more concise.

Do you ~~have knowledge of~~ *know all the legal standards?*

he himself, she herself

Excess ending words. *He* or *she* by themselves will do.

The win was more important than he ~~himself~~ *would admit.*

Name legislation that she ~~herself~~ *was successful at passing.*

hear the sound of

Surplus phrase. The phrase *the sound of* is usually not needed.

Did you hear ~~the sound of~~ *the siren late last night?*

heavy in weight

Overdone. The phrase *in weight* is extra.

With the cast on, his leg was heavy ~~in weight~~.

heir apparent

Redundant. The word *heir* by itself will do.

The ongoing search for an heir ~~apparent~~ *has been futile.*

help and support

Double nouns. Either word will do.

Your help ~~and support~~ *for charity goes unmatched.*

henceforth

Too formal. Try *from now on* or *from now.*

~~Henceforth~~ *from now on, I am not answering any more questions.*

her or his own

The word *own* is excess.
She shared her ~~own~~ experiences with the group.

hidden pitfall

Redundant. If it's a *pitfall*, it implies something being *hidden*.
A ~~hidden~~ pitfall could cost you time and money.

high percentage of

Overblown. The words *most* or *much* say about the same thing.
~~A high percentage of~~ most of us studied Spanish in school.
They're experiencing much ~~a high percentage of~~ turnover.

high time

The word *high* is overstated.
It's ~~high~~ time they started getting paid for back royalties.

historical archive, historical experience, historical past, historical precedent, historical record

Extra word. The word *historical* is not needed in these phrases.
Last year we visited the space program's ~~historical~~ archives.
She reminded me of our ~~historical~~ experience with inflation.
His books rely much on the ~~historical~~ past for inspiration.
The states cited ~~historical~~ precedent for the tax changes.
The ~~historical~~ record of early television remains fuzzy.

hold in abeyance

Time waster. Use the verbs *postpone* or *wait*.
The commission will ~~hold in abeyance~~ postpone any decision.

hold a conference, hold a meeting

Gabby. The verbs *confer* or *meet* are more concise.
The leaders will ~~hold a conference~~ confer in the back room.
When is a good time to ~~hold a meeting~~ meet?

hollow tube

Redundant. All *tubes* are *hollow*.

honest in character, honest truth

Unneeded modifiers.
Nominees for the new position must be honest ~~in character~~.
When it's not complimentary, few like hearing the ~~honest~~ truth.

hopeful optimist

Redundant. An *optimist* is always *hopeful*.
Bob considers himself ~~a hopeful~~ an optimist, not a naysayer.

hopes and aspirations, hopes and desires

Repetition. Choose one or the other but not both.
What are you doing to achieve your ~~hopes and~~ aspirations?
What hopes ~~and desires~~ do you have for the new year?

horrible tragedy, terrible tragedy

Redundant. It's understood *tragedies* are *horrible* or *terrible*.

hostile antagonist

Redundant. An *antagonist* is *hostile*.
Dealing with ~~a hostile~~ (an) antagonist is often impossible.

hot boiling, hot molten metal

The word *hot* is redundant in both phrases.
Oddly, ~~hot~~ boiling water can freeze faster than cold water.
In the factory we could see ~~hot~~ molten metal dripping.

(the) hours of

This phrase is typically not necessary.
The store is open between ~~the hours of~~ 12 and 5 p.m.

huff and puff

Word overkill. One of these words will do.
The consumers may huff ~~and puff~~ over the high prices.

huge conglomerate, huge throng

Redundant. *Conglomerates* and *throngs* are always *huge*.
Typically, ~~huge~~ conglomerates own major TV networks.
A ~~huge~~ throng of fans greeted the celebrity at the hotel.

humongous

Large word. *Big*, *giant*, *huge*, or *large* are simpler word choices.

hundreds and hundreds

Needless ending phrase.

Hundreds ~~and hundreds~~ waited in line for concert tickets.

hurriedly scribbled, scribbled hurriedly

Excess modifiers.

The attorney ~~hurriedly~~ scribbled a note to the judge.

She scribbled ~~hurriedly~~ a note on the hotel stationery.

I

"The way you define yourself as a writer is that you write every time you have a free minute. If you didn't behave that way you would never do anything."—John Irving

I am of the opinion that, I believe that, I feel that, I think that

Usually these personal belief statements can be dropped.
I am of the opinion that we need teamwork to succeed.
I believe that we all want our security and freedom.
Thanks to you, I feel that the fund raiser was successful.
From their reaction, I think that the contest was fair.

I hear what you are saying

The phrase *I understand* is simpler.
I hear what you are saying understand, but I still disagree.

I myself, I personally

Often *myself* and *personally* are extra words.
I myself would not think of doing such a thing.
I personally was at yesterday's announcement.

I thought to myself

Unneeded ending phrase.
When I first heard, I thought(,) to myself what a great idea.

I wish to take this opportunity to thank you

Trim these words to simply *thank you*.
I wish to take this opportunity to thank you for being here.

I would like to

This phrase can typically be removed.
First, I would like to thank you for your work and dedication.

(the) idea that

This phrase can typically be removed.
~~The idea that~~ we could lose tonight is preposterous.

identical match, identical with each other

Needless repeating of the same idea.
The fingerprints are ~~an~~ identical ~~match~~.
Both teams records are identical ~~with each other~~.

identically the same

Redundant. Something *identical* is the *same*.
The cars are ~~identically~~ the same except for horsepower.

if and when

Verbal overload. Either word will do.
If ~~and when~~ the dividend goes, what happens to the stock?

if at all possible

Wordy. The phrase *if possible* is shorter.
If ~~at all~~ possible, the report will be available next month.

if it should happen that, if it should transpire, in the event that, under circumstances in which

Long-winded. Substitute the word *if* for any of these phrases.
~~In the event that~~ if it happens again, report it immediately.

illegal contraband

Redundant. *Contraband* is assumed to be *illegal*.
They're trying to stop the flow of ~~illegal~~ contraband to cities.

illegally smuggled

Redundant. *Smuggling* something is always *illegal*.
Tons of ~~illegally~~ smuggled items arrived at the border.

illustrate

Heavy word for *show*.

immediately adjacent to, immediately adjoining

The phrase *next to* can replace these redundancies.
The ATMs are ~~immediately adjacent~~ next to the hotel.
Suitable parking is ~~immediately adjoining~~ next to the bank.

imminent at any moment

Verbal excess. *Imminent* alone is plenty.
Their arrival is imminent ~~at any moment~~.

immortalized forever

Redundant. If someone is *immortalized*, it's *forever*.
For her caring of the sick, she will be immortalized ~~forever~~.

impartial

Inflated word for *fair* or *just*.

impetuous

Big word for the simpler words *hasty*, *impulsive*, *rash*, or *reckless*.

implement

Lush verb for *apply*, *do,* or *employ.*

implode on itself

Overstated. The word *implode* alone will do.
A few lawmakers feel that industry could implode ~~on itself~~.

important breakthrough, important essential, important VIP

Redundant. All three are understood to be *important*.
A scientist made ~~an important~~ breakthrough in gene research.
Zinc and chromium are ~~important~~ essential nutrients.
They've scheduled ~~an important~~ VIP as the keynote speaker.

improve and enhance

Redundant verbs. One of these words will do.
She wants to ~~improve and~~ enhance the training program.

in a confused state

Word padding. The descriptive word *confused* is plenty.
The council is ~~in a~~ confused ~~state~~ over the new budget.

in a ... direction

At times, this phrase can be omitted.
Make sure to turn the valve ~~in a~~ clockwise ~~direction~~.

in a firm manner, in a hasty manner, in a rapid manner

The adverbs *firmly, hastily,* and *rapidly* are more concise.
He gripped the golf club ~~in a firm manner~~ firmly.
The board made its decision ~~in a hasty manner~~ hastily.
The solvent can clean fabric ~~in a rapid manner~~ rapidly.

in a manner of speaking

This deadwood phrase adds little.
Yes, ~~in a manner of speaking~~, he didn't qualify for the final.

in a number of cases

The shorter phrase *many times* is a crisper option.
~~In a number of cases,~~ many times we did not get feedback.

in a relatively short period of time

Windy. Try substituting the words *quickly* or *soon*.
The coupon expires ~~in a relatively short period of time~~ soon.

in a satisfactory manner, in a similar manner

Roundabout. The words *satisfactorily* and *similarly* are more
direct.
They did their jobs ~~in a satisfactory manner~~ satisfactorily.
Nations will find ways to act ~~in a similar manner~~ similarly.

in a situation in which

The word *when* can sometimes provide the same meaning.
~~In a situation in which~~ when this occurs, try another option.

in a timely manner
Verbose. The words *promptly* or *soon* are much shorter.
Please return your emails ~~in a timely manner~~ promptly.

in a very real sense
At times, this empty phrase can be deleted.
~~In a very real sense,~~ we design machines to help people.

in a westward direction, in a westerly direction
Rambling. Use the words *westward* or *westerly.*
The tornado is moving ~~in a~~ westward ~~direction.~~
The storm is moving ~~in a~~ westerly ~~direction.~~

Note: The same advice applies to *eastward* and *easterly* as well as *downward*, *inward*, *outward*, *upward*, etc.

in accordance with your request, incompliance with your request, pursuant to your request
Legalistic jargon. *As requested* is definitely tighter.
~~Pursuant to your request~~ as requested, here is your refund.

in addition to
Rambling way to say *also*, *and*, or *besides.*
~~In addition to~~ besides eating well, exercise may fight colds.

in advance of
A bit wordy. Use the word *before.*
Schools closed ~~in advance of~~ before the snow arrived.

in all cases
Overdone. The word *always* can sometimes replace this phrase.
This surgery ~~in all cases~~ always involves total rest.

in all likelihood, in all probability
Tedious. The word *perhaps*, *possibly*, or *probably* are simpler.
~~In all likelihood~~ probably we'll receive our grades Monday.
~~In all probability~~ perhaps this is the correct route to travel.

in an area where

Roundabout. The word *where* is more concise.
They bought a house ~~in an area~~ where taxes are low.

in an efficient way

Diluted phrase. The word *efficiently* can replace this phrase.
The program displays data ~~in an efficient way~~ efficiently.

in an effort to

Verbose. Say *to*.
~~In an effort~~ to sell more tickets, prices were reduced.

in anticipation of

Before or *expecting* can say the same thing.
~~In anticipation of~~ expecting frost, the plants were covered.

in association with

Stale phrase. At times, the word *with* is a much simpler replacement.
Our company is working ~~in association~~ with other retailers.

in back of

Chatty. Use the word *behind*.
She's having much pain ~~in back of~~ behind her neck.

in case

Verbal surplus. The simple word *if* is slightly more condensed.
~~In case~~ if you missed it, the film is being re-released soon.

in conjunction with, in connection with

Clutter. Use the preposition *about*.
We know much ~~in connection with~~ about the case.

in consequence of

Stuffy. *Because of* is a less formal phrase to use.
~~In consequence of~~ because of poor planning, things failed.

in consideration of the fact that

Chatty. Say *as*, *because*, or *considering*.
~~In consideration of the fact that~~ because it's new, be careful.

in due course

Excess. Often this phrase can be removed.
~~In due course,~~ we may have meetings to address the issue.

in equal halves

Redundant. The word *equal* is assumed and not needed.
They cut the sheet cake into two ~~equal~~ halves.

in every case, in every instance

Verbose. Say *always*.
~~In every case,~~ they always enjoy vacationing in Maine.

in excess of

Wordy. Use the word *over*.
Your tax refund this year will be ~~in excess of~~ over $1,000.

in fact

Excess. At times, this phrase can be cut.
We have made ~~in fact~~ much progress in optical technology.

in favor of

Overstated. The word *for* is less wordy.
We are ~~in favor of~~ for a higher minimum wage next year.

in height, in length

Overloaded phrasing. Use the words *high* or *long*.
The Colossus of Rhodes stood over 200 feet ~~in height~~ high.
Their new house measures over 60 feet ~~in length~~ long.

in less than no time

Fatty phrase. The word *quickly* is leaner.
She finished her book review ~~in less than no time~~ quickly.

in light of the fact that

Long-winded. Use the word *because*.
~~In light of the fact that~~ because he's late, let's reschedule.

in many cases, in many instances, in most cases, in most instances

Verbose. Say *often* or *usually* for all these phrases.
~~In many cases,~~ usually we offer employee incentives.

in my judgment, in my opinion

Often these personal belief phrases can be omitted.
It's too late ~~in my judgment~~ to start another meeting.
~~In my opinion~~ Blu-ray DVDs have great clarity and sound.

in no case

Fatty phrase. The word *never* is leaner.
I will ~~in no case~~ never consider him for that position.

in no time at all

Roundabout. The word *quickly* is more direct.
He learned the new networking tool ~~in no time at all~~ quickly.

in operation

Excess. Sometimes this phrase can be discarded.
~~In operation~~ the car runs better with a higher octane fuel.

in order for, in order that, in order to

Stale phrases. The words *for*, *so*, or *to* can replace these phrases.
~~In order~~ for this to occur, you will need two signatures.
~~In order that~~ so we don't rush there, we should leave soon.
We applied to that bank ~~in order~~ to get a mortgage.

in place of

Overdone. The word *for* sometimes can be substituted.
Joe will start at first base ~~in place of~~ for the injured Bob.

in point of fact

Wordiness that adds little to a sentence.
In point of fact their role has been known since the 1990s.

in proximity to

Rambling way to say *close to* or *near*.
The housing project is in proximity to near local schools.

in rare cases

Excess. The word *rarely* is more concise.
In rare cases rarely is this treatment ineffective for patients.

in recognition of this fact

Fatty phrase. At times, the word *so* can be a leaner choice.
In recognition of this fact so, we created a position.

in reference to, in regard to, in relation to, in respect to

Extra words. The word *about* can tighten these phrases.
In reference to about your question, doors open at 7 p.m.
She knows something in regard to about the missing items.
The lawyer knows other details in relation to about this case.
They wrote to us in respect to about their financing options.

in response to your letter

Typical business letter phrase that adds little.
In response to your letter your letter indicates....

in shape

Typically this phrase can be removed. Examples include:
The window above the new dormer is conical in shape.
The fruit is oblong in shape and covered with thorns.
The earrings are oval in shape and weigh .45 carats.
Usually the dialog boxes are rectangular in shape.
Generally the structural drawings are spherical in shape.
The bottles holding cologne are typically square in shape.

in short supply

Tedious. The words *scarce* or *sparse* say the same thing.
Special Education teachers are ~~in short supply~~ scarce here.

in size

Excess. When used with words such as *big*, *grow*, *huge*, *large*, *little*, *long*, *short*, and *small*, this phrase can typically be cut.
The new car is smaller ~~in size~~ but more efficient than most.
Her new car is short ~~in size~~ but long on charm.

in some cases, in some instances

Wordy. The word *sometimes* is much crisper for each phrase.
~~In some cases~~, sometimes refinancing is your only option.
~~In some instances~~ sometimes the minutes are not recorded.

in spite of everything to the contrary

Long-winded. Sometimes the word *nevertheless* means the same.
~~In spite of everything to the contrary~~ nevertheless, we went anyway.

in spite of the fact that, despite the fact that

Stale wordy phrases. Use *although*, *despite*, or *even though*.
~~In spite of the fact that~~ despite not having had a hit in years, fans still flock to their concerts.
~~Despite the fact that~~ although we lost, we all played well.

in stature

Overkill. This phrase can usually be discarded when used with words denoting size.
He's not short ~~in stature~~; he's below average height.

in such a way

Overkill. At times, this phrase is unnecessary.
It's built ~~in such a way~~ to withstand strong earthquakes.

in terms of

Verbose. This phrase can often be replaced with other words.
We need to plan what to do ~~in terms of~~ for her birthday.
What are you doing ~~in terms of~~ about these late notices?
Kindness goes a long way ~~in terms of~~ toward helping others.

in that period

Tedious. Use the word *then*.
Back ~~in that period~~ then only certain people could vote.

in the absence of

Long-winded. The word *without* is shorter.
~~In the absence of~~ without solid evidence, you lack a case.

in the amount of

Fatty phrase. The word *for* is leaner.
Last week she received a rebate ~~in the amount of~~ for $75.

in the area of

Lengthy. Typically this phrase can be reduced to the word *in*.
He is an expert in ~~the area of~~ nuclear physics.

in the best of health

Lengthy. A crisper option is the word *healthy*.
They look ~~in the best of health~~ healthy since retirement.

in the context of

A tedious way to say *for* or *in*.
Identity fraud in ~~the context of~~ e-commerce is today's topic.

in the direction of, toward the direction of

Chatty. Say *toward*.
The errant shot headed ~~in the direction of~~ toward the crowd.
The errant shot went toward ~~the direction of~~ the spectators.

in the end

Excess. Often this phrase can be cut.
~~In the end~~, we were not penalized for speaking our minds.

in the final analysis
Wordy. Often this phrase can be deleted.
~~In the final analysis~~ you are better off with this new policy.

in the first place
Rambling way to say *first*.
~~In the~~ first ~~place~~, we want to know what highway to travel.

in the form of
Chatty. Go with the word *as*.
Plants store their carbohydrates ~~in the form of~~ as starch.

in the midst of
Fatty phrase. The words *amid* or *during* are often leaner.
~~In the midst of~~ amid a tough winter, the building continued.
Even ~~in the midst of~~ during snowfall, construction continued.

in the nature of
Verbose. Say *like*.
Something ~~in the nature of~~ like a tax rebate may occur.

in the near future, in the not too distant future
Muddle. Use the word *soon*.
~~In the near future~~ soon our medical benefits will change.
~~In the not too distant future~~ soon the stock price will climb.

in the past
Verbose. At times, the word *over* can replace this phrase.
It's ~~in the past~~ over, so accept the outcome for what it is.

in the process of
Long-winded. This phrase can often be cut.
We are ~~in the process of~~ installing new doors for our house.

in the proximity of
Verbose. Say *near*.
A new hotel is being built ~~in the proximity of~~ near the airport.

in the range of
Rambling. Say *about*, *almost*, *around*, *nearly*, or *roughly*.
Their salaries total ~~in the range of~~ nearly $300,000.

in the recent past
Long-winded. Use the word *recently*.
~~In the recent past~~ recently the company began flex time.

in the time since
Verbal surplus. The word *since* can usually replace this phrase.
~~In the time~~ since your last appraisal, you have done well.

in the vicinity of
Wordy. Use the words *close* or *near*.
Tornadoes are occurring ~~in the vicinity of~~ near that city.

in the way of
Hefty. This phrase can often be cut.
Little was done ~~in the way of~~ getting a bigger server.

in the year .....
Overkill. The phrase *the year* can be omitted.
In ~~the year~~ 2008, some company pension plans were cut.

in this day and age
Trite. The words *currently*, *now*, or *today* can replace this cliché.
Direct contact is done via email ~~in this day and age~~ today.

in those cases
Excess. This phrase can sometimes be removed.
~~In those cases~~ when you have proof, report it immediately.

in today's society
Verbose. At times, the word *today* can replace this phrase.
Technology plays a major role ~~in today's society~~ today.

in total

Unneeded. Often this phrase can be deleted.
He estimates the remodeled kitchen will be $20,000 ~~in total~~.

in view of the above, in view of the fact that, in view of the foregoing

Fatty phrases. The words *because*, *considering*, or *therefore* are leaner choices.
~~In view of the fact that~~ because he didn't study, he failed.

in which

Excess. This phrase often can be deleted.
I cannot see a way ~~in which~~ to vote for the bill.

(has an) inadequate level of

Roundabout. The verb *lacks* is more direct.
Her diet ~~has an inadequate level of~~ lacks protein.

inadvertent error, inadvertent oversight

Overstated. Use the words *error* or *oversight*.
The author apologized for his ~~inadvertent~~ error on page 5.
Because of an ~~inadvertent~~ oversight, we didn't claim the gift.

inadvisable

Bulky word. *Unwise* is a much simpler word.

inasmuch as, insofar as

Chatty. Use the preposition *because*.
~~Inasmuch as~~ because this is a first draft, expect comments.
~~Insofar as~~ because he is a witness, his testimony is key.

inaugurate

Posh word. The verb *begin* is simpler.

inception

Big word for the simpler word *start*.

included as part of every

Extra words. The phrase *included in every* is briefer.
Included ~~as part of~~ in every VIP package is a parking pass.

includes but not limited to

Overstated. Just the verb *includes* is plenty.
Personal data includes ~~but not limited to~~ name and town.

includes a discussion on, includes reference to

Clutter. Use the verbs *discusses* or *refers*.
Her cookbook ~~includes a discussion on~~ discusses vegan diets.
The book ~~includes reference to~~ refers to economic theories.

(the) inclusion of

Stilted. The word *including* is a better choice.
The new law led to ~~the inclusion of~~ including all under 18.

incombustible

Showy word. The words *fireproof* or *flameproof* are simpler.

income coming in

Excessive. The noun *income* by itself will do.
She has income ~~coming in~~ from other rental properties.

incorporate

Bulky verb for *include.*

(an) increasing proportion of

Stuffy. The word *more* can replace this phrase.
~~An increasing proportion of~~ more imports are arriving daily.

increasingly more

The adverb *increasingly* is not needed.
Heart disease is ~~increasingly~~ more common in adults.

incremental stages

Redundant. *Stages* are always *incremental.*
The construction inspections occur at ~~incremental~~ stages.

incubation period

Overdone. Drop the word *period*.
The incubation ~~period~~ should last for two more weeks.

inculcate

Large word. Try the simpler words *instill* or *repeat*.

indebtedness

The simpler word *debt* says the same thing.

indeterminate

Inflated word for *vague*.

indicate

Prefer the simple word *show*.

indicted on a charge

Redundant. When one is *indicted*, a *charge* follows.
They were indicted ~~on a charge~~ for investment fraud.

indigent poor

Redundant. *Indigent* means being *poor*.
The ~~indigent~~ poor represent a good part of the population.

individual person

Redundant. Every *person* is an *individual*.
Each child is an individual ~~person~~ with a unique personality.

indoctrinate

Weighty word for *instruct* or *teach*.

inexpensive and cheap

Redundant adjectives. Choose one or the other but not both.
A(n) ~~inexpensive and~~ cheap service hosts our website.

infrequent

Hefty word for *rare* or *seldom*.

inherent to

Sometimes the word *of* can replace this phrase.
This is viewed as a risk ~~inherent to~~ of e-business.

initial

Plush word. *First* is a much simpler word.

initial beginning, initial breakthrough, initial introduction, initial start

The modifier *initial* is often uncalled for in these phrases.
From the ~~initial~~ beginning, we thought the plan would work.
Since the vaccine's ~~initial~~ breakthrough, lives were saved.
After his ~~initial~~ introduction last year, he played like a pro.
She received her ~~initial~~ start in an off Broadway play.

(the) initial task will be to

The word *first* could replace this phrase.
~~The initial task will be to~~ first prove it works before I buy it.

initiate

Begin or *start* are less stuffy words.

inner core, inner feeling

Word overkill. The word *inner* can be dropped.
Earth's ~~inner~~ core begins 4,000 miles beneath the crust.
We had a strange ~~inner~~ feeling we were being watched.

innocent bystander

Redundant. *Bystanders* are assumed to be *innocent*.
Luckily the ~~innocent~~ bystander was there to aid the victim.

innovation

Inflated word for *change* or *new*.

inquire

Lush word. The word *ask* is simpler.

inside of, outside of

Often *of* is an unessential preposition.
We'll return the completed questionnaire inside ~~of~~ a week.
If you travel outside ~~of~~ the U.S., you'll need immunizations.

insignificant and unimportant

Verbal surplus. One of these words will do.
What he said is by no means insignificant ~~and unimportant~~.

insofar as this is concerned

The phrase *as for this* is simpler.
~~Insofar as this is concerned~~ as for this, we can resolve it.

instigate

Big word for the simpler words *begin, start*, or *urge*.

institute

Begin, introduce, or *start* are simpler word choices.

institute a change to

The verb *change* is plenty.
As a result, we will ~~institute a~~ change ~~to~~ our process.

insufficient

Weighty word for *lacking* or *not enough*.

(an) integral part of

At times, the phrase *an integral* can be omitted.
They are ~~an integral~~ part of the company's success.

integrated with each other

Unneeded repeating of the same idea.
The financial systems are not integrated ~~with each other~~.

intentional arson, intentional fraud, intentional planning

Redundant. *Arson*, *fraud*, and *planning* are *intentional*.
The fire investigators concluded it was ~~intentional~~ arson.
The Circuit Court jury found he committed ~~intentional~~ fraud.
The ~~intentional~~ planning let us identify new requirements.

interact with each other

Often unnecessary ending phrase.
Participants can interact ~~with each other~~ via a text chat.

interactive dialogue

Redundant. *Dialogue* has to be *interactive*.
After the meeting, time was allotted for ~~interactive~~ dialogue.

interdependent on each other

Interdependent alone will do.
People are interdependent ~~on each other~~ for new ideas.

interest and concern

Double nouns. Either word will do.
We appreciate your interest ~~and concern~~ for our family.

interpose no objection to

The word *approve* can replace this legalistic jargon.
The board ~~interposes no objection to~~ approves the project.

interrogate

Prefer familiar verbs like *ask*, *grill*, or *question*.

interval of time

Extra words. The word *interval* will do.
Our server is crashing at regular intervals ~~of time~~.
See also entry for **time interval**.

intimate (verb)

Hint, *say*, or *suggest* are simpler.

intrepid

Bold, *brave*, *daring*, or *heroic* are simpler word choices.

intrinsic

Bulky word for *basic*, *real*, or *true*.

introduced a new, introduced for the first time

Pointless ending words.
He introduced a ~~new~~ bill to study possible misconduct.
They were introduced ~~for the first time~~ the other day.

intuitively obvious

Redundant. If it's *intuitive*, it's *obvious*.
It is ~~intuitively~~ obvious to even the most casual observer.

invited guest

Redundant. All *guests* are *invited*.
She has been ~~an invited~~ guest lecturer at many colleges.

involve the necessity of

Wordy. The words *demand* or *require* are shorter.
Field trips usually ~~involve the necessity of~~ require a report.

involves the use of

Windy. The words *employs* or *uses* are crisper.
Physical therapy often ~~involves the use of~~ uses light weights.

inward

Occasionally, we can simply use the word *in*.
As the antennas are moved in~~ward~~, the reception is better.

inward into

Occasionally, we can simply use the word *into*.
Cells can move ~~inward~~ into the muscle and form new tissue.

ironically enough

Overkill. The word *enough* usually can be deleted.
Ironically ~~enough~~, they easily won without their star player.

irrespective of

Complex way to simply say *despite* or *even if*.
Asthma has increased ~~irrespective of~~ despite cleaner air.

is a person who

Clutter. This phrase can typically be cut.
Joe ~~is a person who~~ always gets excellent feedback.

is (are) able to, is (are) capable of

Exchange these wordy phrases for the word *can*.
John ~~is able to~~ can help you with your taxes this year.
Our antenna ~~is capable of~~ can pick~~ing~~ up HD signals.

is (are) an aid to

Lengthy. The word *helps* is much shorter.
Exercise ~~is an aid to~~ helps fight high cholesterol levels.

is (are) applicable to

Verbose. Use the phrase *applies to*.
The new policy ~~is applicable to~~ applies to all workers.

is (are) at variance with

Too complex. The phrase *differs with* is much simpler.
What he told the law ~~is at variance~~ differs with the facts.

is (are) aware of

See entry for **be aware of, was aware of**.

is (are) characterized by

Fatty phrase. The words *has* or *resembles* are leaner.
The Orlando area ~~is characterized by~~ has great weather.

is (are) comprised of

Roundabout. The word *contains* is more direct.
The book ~~is comprised of~~ contains 20 chapters.

is (are) dependent on

Too complex. The phrase *depends on* is simpler.
Her success ~~is dependent~~ depends on her overall attitude.

is (are) designed to be, is (are) designed to run

Wordy. The words *is* or *runs* are much more concise choices.
This course is ~~designed to be~~ an introduction for engineers.
Her new car ~~is designed to~~ runs on higher octane fuel.

is (are) desirous of

Overstated. The word *wants* is crisper.
The city ~~is desirous of~~ wants something better for its people.

is equipped with

Wordy. The word *has* can replace this phrase.
The new car ~~is equipped with~~ has satellite radio.

is helpful in understanding

Wordy. The verb *clarifies* can sometimes replace this phrase.
His talk ~~is helpful in understanding~~ clarifies the medical plan.

is in a position to

Wordy. Try to go with only the word *can*.
The company ~~is in a position to~~ can now provide healthcare.

is (are) in accordance with

Wordy. The phrase *agree with* is shorter.
The new rule ~~is in accordance~~ agrees with the voters.

is (are) in contrasts to

Wordy. The phrase *contrasts with* is simpler.
That belief ~~is in~~ contrasts ~~to~~ with other popular religions.

is (are) in violation with
Wordy. The word *violates* is more concise.
That ~~is in violation of~~ violates Section 5 of the housing code.

is (are) lacking in
Wordy. The word *lacks* is simpler.
Their high protein diet ~~is lacking in~~ lacks a few vitamins.

is (are) looking for
Wordy. At times, the verb *needs* is briefer.
He ~~is looking for~~ needs an expert attorney on this case.

is (are) reflective of
Wordy. *Reflect* or *resemble* are more concise.
The new regulations ~~is reflective of~~ reflect the bureaucracy.

is (are) scared of
Overstated. The word *fears* is shorter.
The incumbent ~~is scared of~~ fears losing in the primaries.

is (are) seen as
Wordy. The word *is* can replace this phrase.
For some, computer animation is ~~seen as~~ a work of art.

is (are) used for, is (are) used to
Often these phrases can be cut through verb agreement.
This tool **is used for** sending files. vs. This tool **sends** files.
This option **is used to** search ... vs. This option **searches** ...

is (are) when
Weak construction and wordy. Try dropping it.
In the second month ~~is when~~ things are always hectic at work.

it cannot be denied that
Verbose. The word *undeniably* is crisper.
~~It cannot be denied that~~ undeniably, climate change is real.

it could happen that

Word padding. At times, this phrase can be discarded.
It could happen that you may be asked to speak next.

it goes without saying

Overkill. If *it goes without saying*, why say it?
It goes without saying we have more goals than last year.

it has been found that, it has been said that,
it has long been known that

These deadwood phrases usually add nothing.
It has been found that proper sleep can add to longevity.
It has been said that people who exercise often sleep well.
It has long been known that the sun provides vitamin D.

it is (or it was)

These weak constructions, coupled with *that* or *who*, can be removed.
It is his last film that shows his genius best.
It is the manager who signs and sends our checks.

Sometimes the phrase can be cut.
It is necessary that we must take a stand on the issues.
It is possible that soy powder may lower serum cholesterol.

Other times leaner words can replace the fatty phrase.
It is incumbent upon us to we should discuss the issue.
It is recommended that you should study the effects first.

Other possibilities (with their substitutes) include:

it is a fact that – we know
it is advisable to – you should
it is apparent that – apparently
it is clear that – clearly
it is compulsory – you must
it is crucial that – you must or should
it is evident that – evidently
it is imperative – be sure
it is important that – you must

it is important to remember – remember
it is interesting to note that – note
it is not necessary that – you need not
it is noted that – note
it is obligatory – you must
it is obvious that – obviously
it is often the case - often
it is our intention – we intend
it is our opinion – we think
it is probable that – probably
it is recognized that – we know
it is well known that – we know

it may be said that, it seems that

These deadwood phrases add nothing.
~~It may be said that~~ Plato's work is up for interpretation.
~~It seems that~~ some could be allergic to aspartame.

it may well be that

Wordy. *Perhaps* is much shorter.
~~It may well be that~~ perhaps the students were confused.

it's not rocket science

Overused cliché meaning *not difficult*. Avoid.

it should be noted, it should be understood

Wordy. The verbs *note* or *understand* can replace these phrases.
~~It should be noted~~ note that this data comes from research.
~~It should be understood~~ understand that it's not a cure all.

it should not be forgotten that

Rambling. Use the verb *remember*.
~~It should not be forgotten that~~ remember he did much for us.

it stands to reason that

Empty expression. It can often be omitted.
~~It stands to reason that~~ if we leave now, we'll beat the traffic.

it will be necessary to

Wordy. *I must*, *we must*, or *you must* are better options.
It will be necessary to I must upgrade the anti-virus software.

it would appear that, it would seem that

Long-winded. The words *apparently* or *probably* are simpler.
It would appear that apparently the disease is genetic.
It would seem that probably we were wrong about them.

it would be advisable to

Word padding. The phrase *you should* is more personal and concise.
It would be advisable to you should try to eat a balanced diet.

J

"Do not accustom yourself to use big words for little matters."—
Samuel Johnson

jet plane
Redundant. A *jet* is a *plane*.
We've been traveling by jet ~~plane~~ for over 40 years.

Jewish rabbi, Jewish synagogue
Redundant. *Rabbis* and *synagogues* are from the Jewish faith.

joint
Sometimes an uncalled-for introductory word.
We improved the ~~joint~~ cooperation between the companies.

Other possibilities to consider include:

joint agreement
joint collaboration
joint co-sponsorship
joint partnership

judicious
Inflated word for *astute*, *careful*, *shrewd*, or *wise*.

jurisdiction
Command, *control*, or *power* are much simpler words.

just about
About, *almost*, and *nearly* can replace this phrase.
~~Just about~~ almost everyone in the group attended the party.

just barely, just exactly, just merely, just simply, just precisely, just recently

Redundant modifiers. The word *just* is excess.
It ~~just~~ barely qualified as an accredited institution.
The store had ~~just~~ exactly what we were looking for.
She was ~~just~~ merely pointing to a fact we almost overlooked.
People who do not like this idea are ~~just~~ simply wrong.
~~Just~~ precisely how much time is invested in this research?
I ~~just~~ recently finished my first semester of teaching online.

Note: Sentences are usually stronger without the word *just*.
We ~~just~~ thought we would stop by to see how you are.
I'm ~~just~~ writing to ask if you will be available tomorrow.
If you would ~~just~~ email me all the items you need.

justify and explain

Redundant verbs. Choose one or the other but not both.
The auditor failed to ~~justify and~~ explain the cost overruns.

K

"Use familiar words—words that your readers will understand, and not words they will have to look up."—James J. Kilpatrick

keep in mind

Chatty. The word *remember* is more concise.
~~Keep in mind~~ remember, you may not get another chance.

keep track of

Wordy. The simple verb *track* is more to the point.
The web-based tool is a good way to ~~keep~~ track ~~of~~ your bills.

kind of

Extra words. Omit this phrase when possible.
Citizens carefully watched the ~~kind of~~ new proposed polices.

kindly arrange to send

Overstated. The phrase *arrange to* is unnecessary.
Kindly ~~arrange to~~ send our regrets to your family and friends.

kitty cat

Redundant. A *kitty* is a *cat*.
The children adopted a kitty ~~cat~~ from the local shelter.

knots per hour

Redundant. *Knots* implies *per hour*.
The ship could travel at 20 knots ~~per hour~~.

know about

See entry for **average about, debate about**.

know for a fact

Wordy. The word *know* is more concise.
We know ~~for a fact~~ that many minor accidents go unreported.

knowledgeable expert

Redundant. *Experts* are always *knowledgeable*.
Our ~~knowledgeable~~ experts can help you design a new system.

known by the name of

Rambling. The word *named* can replace this phrase.
The dog was ~~known by the name of~~ named Winchester.

known fact

Redundant. *Facts* are always *known*.
It's a ~~known~~ fact oatmeal may help reduce high cholesterol.

L

"In character, in manner, in style, in all things, the supreme excellence is simplicity."—Henry Wadsworth Longfellow

lacerations
Overweight word. Try the word *cuts*.

lack the ability to
Rambling. Pare this phrase to simply *cannot*.
Humans ~~lack the ability to~~ cannot make Vitamin C.

lag behind
See entry for **follow behind, leave behind, trail behind**.

large amount of
Chatty. The word *much* is crisper.
~~Large amount of~~ much flu vaccine is needed this year.

large in size
The category of size is already implied. Delete *in size*.
From the MRI, the tumor appeared large ~~in size~~.

large mansion, large urban center
Unneeded modifiers. *Mansion* and *urban center* imply *large*.
The Vanderbilts owned a ~~large~~ mansion in Hyde Park, N.Y.
Three of the ~~large~~ urban centers in the study are in Florida.

(a) large number of, (a) large percentage of, (a) large proportion of
Overblown way to say *many* or *most*.
~~A large number of~~ many pesticides were recently banned.
~~A large percentage of~~ most students passed the exam.
~~A large proportion of~~ most graduates are entering college.

large scale

Go with the word *large*.
We're readying large ~~scale~~ moves into solar power.

large-sized

The word *sized* is not needed.
The dermatologist found large-~~sized~~ moles on her back.

last and final

Overstated. Either word will do.
It was the team's ~~last and~~ final offer before arbitration.

last but not least

The word *finally* can replace this well-worn phrase.
~~Last but not least~~ finally, a special thanks to my parents.

last farewell

Redundant. All *farewells* are *last*.
He bid a ~~last~~ farewell to those who supported his candidacy.

last of all

The words *finally* or *lastly* are plenty.
And ~~last of all~~ finally, please meet our newest member, Tim.

last swan song

See entry for **farewell swan song, final swan song**.

lasting and permanent

Repetition. Choose one or the other but not both.
Her business wants ~~lasting and~~ permanent customer value.

lasting legacy

Redundant. A *legacy* is *lasting*.
He's leaving a ~~lasting~~ legacy fit for future generations.

later on

Verbal surplus. *On* is an unessential ending preposition.
Studies show viruses in babies may cause asthma later ~~on~~.

laughing out loud, talking out loud

Wordy. The phrase *out loud* can be removed.
The students were caught laughing ~~out loud~~ in class.
Most libraries prohibit talking ~~out loud~~ in the corridors.

learned scholar

Redundant. All *scholars* are *learned*.
He is a ~~learned~~ scholar, wise counselor, and superb teacher.

leave behind

*See entry for **follow behind, lag behind, trail behind**.*

leaving out of consideration

Overstated. Use the words *ignoring* or *disregarding*.
You're ~~leaving out of consideration~~ ignoring all the facts.

left-hand, left-hand side

Extra word. The word *hand* is not needed.
You need to take a left ~~hand~~ turn at the next intersection.
Make your comments on the left ~~hand~~ side of the page.

level to the ground

Wordy. Trim this phrase to the verb *level*.
The demolition will level ~~to the ground~~ the old buildings.

light in weight

Wordy. The phrase *in weight* is not needed.
Without the cast on, his leg was light ~~in weight~~.

limitation

Inflated word for *limit*.

limited number of

Rambling. Use the word *few*.
A ~~limited number~~ few ~~of~~ tickets are available for the play.

limits and restrictions
Redundant nouns. Choose one or the other but not both.
All donors are subject to limits and restrictions.

linger on
Tedious. *Linger* alone will do.
The odor from the factory tends to linger on at night.

liquidate
Stuffy word for *annul* or *clear*.

literally
Muddle. This qualifier seldom adds anything.
Mary is literally the smartest person we've ever hired.

literate readers
Unneeded modifier. Delete the word *literate*.
Her new book could be a hit with many literate readers.

little
Unneeded modifier when used with words implying *little*.
They were born in a little hamlet in upstate New York.
In 1976 the company released its popular little infant doll.

Other examples to consider include:

little bit	little morsel
little detail	little particle
little duckling	little sapling
little dwarf	little shred
little fraction	little smidgen
little fragment	little speck
little hint	little tiny
little in stature	little trace
little iota	

(a) little-known esoteric
Redundant. *Esoteric* already implies *little-known*.
The inhabitants spoke a little-known an esoteric language.

(a) little less than

Clutter. Use the word *almost*.
In a little less than almost an hour, the program will start.

live audience, live witness

Redundant. *Audiences* and *witnesses* are *live*.
The show was taped before a live studio audience.
The trial will require many live witnesses to testify.

local neighbor, local resident, local vernacular

Redundant. All three words imply something being *local*.
Our local neighbor is having a garage sale next week.
He was among the local residents who received a tax break.
He has no problem understanding the local vernacular there.

locality, location

Large words for the simpler words *areas, places,* or *sites*.

located

Verbal surplus. Quite often this word can be deleted.
The grammar school was located in an old part of the city.

lodge a complaint with

Long-winded. Try the phrase *complain to*.
I will lodge a complaint with complain to the hotel's front desk.

lonely isolation

Redundant. *Isolation* is *lonely*.
Before being found, the dog had days of lonely isolation.

long and protracted

Both words imply *long*; choose only one.
Last year we had a long and protracted contract negotiation.

long chronic illness

Repetition. Use either *long illness* or *chronic illness* but not both.
Even with a long chronic illness, one can live to be 100.

long enduring, long litany

Word overkill. The word *long* can be dropped.
In Star Trek, the Klingons have some ~~long~~ enduring customs.
A ~~long~~ litany of allegations have surfaced the last two weeks.

look ahead to the future

Extra words. The phrase *to the future* is unnecessary.
The storm victims will look ahead ~~to the future~~ and rebuild.

looking back in hindsight, looking back in retrospect

Chatty. The phrase *looking back* is not needed.
Probably ~~looking back~~ in hindsight, we made a mistake.
~~Looking back~~ in retrospect, I'm glad I have my degree.

looming bad

Repetition. Go with either *looming* or *bad* but not both.
The residents were not warned of the looming ~~bad~~ weather.

loquacious

Stuffy word for *talkative* or *wordy*.

(a) lot of

Chatty. Say *many* or *much*.

loudly

Often this adverb can be cut when used with a word already
implying something *loud*.
When children yell ~~loudly~~, they often get people's attention.

Other possibilities to consider include:

bellow loudly	screech loudly
holler loudly	shout loudly
roar loudly	shriek loudly
scream loudly	

lowly downtrodden

Redundant modifier. The word *lowly* can be deleted.
The crowd abandoned the ~~lowly~~ downtrodden outcasts.

M

"To write simply is as difficult as to be good."—Somerset Maugham

made a statement saying
Long-winded. The words *said* or *stated* will do.
The judge ~~made a statement saying~~ said the verdict is in.

main focus
Unessential modifier.
Conciseness is the ~~main~~ focus of this writing class.

maintain cost control
Wordy. The word *maintain* is not needed.
They want to improve service and ~~maintain~~ control cost.

major breakthrough, major protagonist
Major is a redundant modifier in these phrases.
The discovery was a ~~major~~ breakthrough in astronomy.
The book suffers from the lack of any ~~major~~ protagonist.

(a) major portion of, (a) majority of
Fatty phrases. The words *many*, *most*, or *much of* are leaner.
Flooding has closed ~~a major portion of~~ most of the highway.
~~A majority~~ many favor the confirmation of the new judge.

make a, make an
These phrases can lead to wordiness and nominalizations. By exposing the *true verb* in a phrase, you can add action to your writing (with fewer words).
The company will ~~make attempts~~ attempt to contact them.
I will ~~make an inquiry regarding~~ ask about the late payment.
We will ~~make~~ mention ~~of~~ her name as a good replacement.
We can always ~~make~~ use ~~of~~ more technical help.

Here are other "make" phrases with their *true verbs*.

make a conclusion – conclude
make a decision – decide
make a determination – determine
make a discovery – discover
make a discussion – discuss
make a distinction – distinguish
make a judgment – judge
make a movement – move
make a notification – notify
make a proposal – propose
make a reaction – react
make a recommendation – recommend
make a report – report
make a selection – select
make a solution – solve
make a statement – state
make a summary – summarize
make a visitation – visit
make an adjustment – adjust
make an agreement – agree
make an analysis – analyze
make an announcement – announce
make an appearance – appear
make an application – apply
make an approach – approach
make an approximation – approximate
make an assessment – assess
make an assumption – assume
make an end – end
make an estimate – estimate
make an evaluation – evaluate
make an examination of – examine
make an exception of – except
make an explanation – explain
make an investigation – investigate
make allowance for – allow for
make changes to – change

make contact with – contact or meet
make for the inclusion of – include
make mention of – mention
make preparation for – prepare
make provision for – provide
make reference to – refer
make the acquaintance – acquaint
make the distinction – distinguish

Note: Other introductory verbs like *perform, present, provide,*
and *reach* form similar diluted phrases that hide the true verb.

malodorous stench

Redundant. Any *stench* is *malodorous.*
The flower will soon bloom and emit its ~~malodorous~~ stench.

manifested

Complex verb. Go with the simpler verb *shown.*

manipulate

Inflated verb. *Control* or *handle* are simpler verbs.

(the) manner in which

Verbose. Use the word *how.*
~~The manner in which~~ how chemicals are disposed is critical.

manually by hand

Redundant. If it's done *by hand*, it's *manually* done.
Some camera lenses let you focus manually ~~by hand~~.

manufacture

Big verb. Try the simpler verb *make.*

many and varied

Verbose. The word *multiple* can replace this phrase.
I use an accountant for multiple ~~many and varied~~ reasons.

many but not all, some but not all
Overstated. Use *many* or *some*.
Many ~~but not all~~ tellers are sold on a new banking system.
The new spam filter rejects some ~~but not all~~ emails.

many different people, many different things
Word overkill. Drop the word *different* from these phrases.
Marketing means many things to many ~~different~~ people.
People do many ~~different~~ things to stay alert and healthy.

many frequent
Repetition. Choose one word or the other but not both.
The college offers many ~~frequent~~ leadership workshops.

marginal
Showy word. Try the simpler words *slight* or *small*.

markedly distinct
Meaningless intensifier. Omit *markedly*.
Their grammar is ~~markedly~~ distinct from other languages.

mass epidemic, mass exodus, mass extinction
Overkill. The adjective *mass* is unneeded.
It appears ~~a mass~~ an epidemic of shingles may break out.
The continued hurricanes account for the ~~mass~~ exodus.
Not many years ago, the bison was near ~~mass~~ extinction.

match exactly (or perfectly)
Word overkill. The word *match* by itself is plenty.
The credit card billing and shipping addresses match ~~exactly~~.

materialize
Big word. Try the simpler words *appear*, *develop*, or *occur*.

(a) matter of urgency
Chatty. Just say *urgent*.
Her doctor's appointment is ~~a matter of urgency~~ urgent.

maximize and optimize

Redundant verbs. Choose one or the other but not both.
Advertising can maximize ~~and optimize~~ business success.

maximum amount, maximum limit

Redundant. A *maximum* is an *amount* or *limit*.
What is the maximum ~~amount~~ I can withdraw from the ATM?
My 401K plan has a maximum ~~limit~~ of what I can contribute.

may in the future

Rambling. Try using *could*, *may*, or *might*.
We may ~~in the future~~ have another meeting on this topic.

may or may not, may perhaps, may possibly, may potentially

Wordy. Just the word *may* is plenty.
John may ~~or may not~~ join us on vacation this summer.
Their platform may ~~perhaps~~ interest some new voters.
The findings may ~~possibly~~ be a cure for the disease.
The transmitter may ~~potentially~~ interfere with our signal.

mean it sincerely

Tedious. The adverb *sincerely* is excess.
You're a lovely group of people, and I mean it ~~sincerely~~.

meanders back and forth

Verbose. The verb *meanders* by itself is plenty.
The stream meanders ~~back and forth~~ across its floodplain.

meaningless gibberish

Redundant. *Gibberish* is always *meaningless*.
The manuscript contains some ~~meaningless~~ gibberish.

meet head on, meet up with

Muddle. The simple verb *meet* will often do here.
The two teams will meet ~~head on~~ in the championship game.
They plan to meet ~~up with~~ other fans at the convention.

meets with our approval

Rambling. A roundabout way to say *we approve*.
If your product meets with our approval, we will list it.

vs.

If we approve your product, we will list it.

memorable impression

Redundant. All *impressions* are *memorable*.
Her writing leaves ~~a memorable~~ an impression on readers.

mental attitude, mental telepathy

Redundant. *Attitude* and *telepathy* relate to a mental state.
Remember to maintain a positive ~~mental~~ attitude on the job.
Research shows some animals can do ~~mental~~ telepathy.

merge into one

Overdone. Use the verb *merge*.
In a few miles, the two lanes merge ~~into one~~.

meticulous

Bulky word. Try the simpler words *careful*, *exact*, or *fussy*.

microscopic bacteria

Redundant. *Bacteria* is always *microscopic*.
They recently detected ~~microscopic~~ bacteria in the water.

(the) midnight hour

Overstated. Use the word *midnight* by itself.
I plan on leaving here at ~~the~~ midnight ~~hour~~.

midway between

Chatty. The word *between* by itself is plenty.
The inn is almost ~~midway~~ between the ski slopes and town.

might or might not, might perhaps, might possibly, might potentially

Wordy. Go with just the word *might*.
She might ~~or might not~~ be available for the rest of the day.
A software upgrade might ~~perhaps~~ fix the problem.
This new lawsuit might ~~possibly~~ involve plagiarism.
Regular exercise might ~~potentially~~ help one's stamina.

miles in distance

Verbose. The word *miles* by itself is plenty.
Two inches on the map represents 300 miles ~~in distance~~.

minimize as far as possible

Long-winded. *Minimize* by itself is enough.
The drug will minimize ~~as far as possible~~ any side effects.

minimum amount, minimum limit

Redundant. A *minimum* is an *amount* or a *limit*.
What's the minimum ~~amount~~ I can contribute to an IRA?
The bank raised the minimum ~~limit~~ for credit card payments.

(a) minimum of

Wordy. *At least* is shorter, but often the phrase can be omitted.
We need ~~a minimum of~~ at least two hours to prepare our task.
The temperature ranges from ~~a minimum of~~ 5 to 20 degrees.

minuscule

Big word. Try the simpler words *little* or *tiny*.

minutely detail

Tedious. The verb *detail* alone will do.
The book ~~minutely~~ details his training and coaching methods.

misleading and false

Redundant adjectives. Choose one or the other but not both.
He gave false ~~and misleading~~ testimony during the hearing.

misleading lie
Redundant. Every *lie* is *misleading*.
The ~~misleading~~ lie cost many people all their life savings.

missing gaps
Redundant. *Gaps* are assumed to be *missing*.
She's trying to identify the ~~missing~~ gaps in his testimony.

mitigate
Stuffy word. *Ease*, *lessen*, *moderate*, or *soften* are simpler.

mix and mingle
Redundant verbs. Choose one or the other but not both.
They chose to mix ~~and mingle~~ with the guests before dinner.

modern state-of-the-art
Redundant. *Modern* means *state-of-the-art*.
The multimedia lab has modern ~~state-of-the-art~~ equipment.

modification
Large word. Try the simpler noun *change*.

moist fog, damp fog
Redundant. All fogs are *moist* or *damp*.

(a) moment in time
Excessive. Use the phrase *a moment*.
The photographer superbly captured a moment ~~in time~~.

monetary fine, monetary funding
Unneeded modifiers. Delete the word *monetary*.
The penalty for violating the statute is a small ~~monetary~~ fine.
The alumni needs ~~monetary~~ funding for the new scholarship.

monetary resources
Chatty. The words *assets*, *capital*, *cash*, or *money* are simpler.
More business will mean more ~~monetary resources~~ capital.

money-back refund

Redundant modifying phrase. *Refund* should be by itself.
How do we apply for the 30-day ~~money-back~~ refund?

(the) month of

Rambling. This phrase can typically be discarded.
Next year we graduate in ~~the month of~~ May.

more easier, more improved, more perfect, more preferable, more superior

In certain contexts, the word *more* should not be a qualifier.
My former job was ~~more~~ easier than my current job.
The new offices had a(n) ~~more~~ improved ventilation system.
He sought ~~more~~ perfect solutions to resolve the challenges.
Your first choice is ~~more~~ preferable to all the others.
Some feel martial arts are ~~more~~ superior to boxing.

more or less, basically

Wordy. These phrases often can be deleted.
The software is becoming ~~more or less~~ obsolete.
To say hybrid cars are not selling well is ~~basically~~ untrue.

more than one

Chatty. Use the word *multiple*.
We know ~~more than one~~ multiple ways to invest wisely.

morning sunrise

Redundant. *Sunrises* are in the *morning*.
She captured a beautiful ~~morning~~ sunrise with her camera.

most especially, most likely, most probably

Verbal surplus. The word *most* is often not needed.
The play was superb, ~~most~~ especially the performances.
Drilling for gas ~~most~~ likely caused the volcano's eruption.
The source of infection was ~~most~~ probably the hospital.

most favorite

Overdone. The word *most* is not needed.
Of all their music, what is your ~~most~~ favorite Beatles song?

most recent

Fatty phrase. The words *latest* or *newest* are leaner.
You can find the ~~most recent~~ latest updates at our website.

moving river, moving stream

Redundant. All *rivers* and *streams* move.
The rafters were caught in a swift ~~moving~~ river (or stream).

multitudinous

Large word. *Countless* or *infinite* are simpler word choices.

(a) must

Tired phrase we can avoid.
This a must film to see. vs. *Everyone should see this film.*

must inevitably

Extra word. At times, the adjective *must* is not needed.
Darwin argued animals ~~must~~ inevitably build a moral sense.

mutual

Unneeded modifier in phrases such as:
Both parties agreed to end the contract by ~~mutual~~ consent.
Their ~~mutual~~ dependence may have an unexpected outcome.

Other examples to consider include:

mutual agreement	mutual friendship
mutual communication	mutual relationship
mutual confidence	mutual respect
mutual cooperation	mutual understanding

mutual advantage to both

Wordy. The phrase *to both* can be removed.
The new proposal is of mutual advantage ~~to both~~.

my own personal, my personal opinion

Word overkill. The adjective *personal* can be omitted.

I have my own ~~personal~~ view on the city budget.

In my ~~personal~~ opinion, the termination was unjustified.

N

"The pages are still blank, but there is a miraculous feeling of the words being there, written in invisible ink and clamoring to become visible."—Vladimir Nabokov

narrower in width

Excess. The phrase *in width* is not needed.
The new cars are shorter and narrower ~~in width~~ this year.

native habitat

Overdone. The adjective *native* is not necessary.
Removing the animal from its ~~native~~ habitat is a mistake.

natural attrition, natural herb, natural instinct, naturally inherent

Redundant modifier. Omit the words *natural* and *naturally*.
~~Natural~~ attrition is cutting public service jobs.
We take many ~~natural~~ herbs for better health and healing.
Our ~~natural~~ instincts always tend toward healthy lives.
Caffeine is ~~naturally~~ inherent to this herb.

near facsimile, near proximity

Overstated. Omit the word *near*.
Photocopies can make a ~~near~~ facsimile of the original item.
Restaurants are plentiful in the ~~near~~ proximity of the hotel.

neat and tidy

Redundant adjectives. Choose one or the other but not both.
Her website is well organized, easy to use, and neat ~~and tidy.~~

nebulous

Inflated word for *hazy* or *vague*.

necessary essential, necessary need, necessary requirement, necessary requisite

The word *necessary* is redundant here.

The class covers the ~~necessary~~ essentials of leadership.
The teacher explained the ~~necessary~~ need for a new edition.
A dissertation is a ~~necessary~~ requirement for your doctorate.
Ethical conduct is a ~~necessary~~ requisite in their company.

necessitate

A posh word for *compel*, *demand*, *need*, or *require*.

(a) necessity for

Wordy. The words *must* or *should* are better choices.

Innovation is a ~~necessity for~~ must for our team's success.

needless and unnecessary

Redundant adjectives. Choose one or the other but not both.

We care about today's ~~needless and~~ unnecessary suffering.

needless to say

Overkill. If it's *needless to say*, why say it?

Anyway, ~~needless to say,~~ this story left many confused.

negative

Needless modifier in certain phrases.

Weak sales is one ~~negative~~ misfortune that's hurt us.

Other possibilities to consider include *negative no* and *negative stigma*.

negative input

Wordy. The word *complaint* is more concise.

We received ~~negative inputs~~ complaints on the fund raising.

negligible

Heavy word for *small* or *tiny*.

neither one

Chatty. Use the word *neither*.
Though we studied both ideas, neither ~~one~~ was adopted.

never at any time, never before in the past

Roundabout. The word *never* is more direct.
They were never ~~at any time~~ in jeopardy of losing the game.
Never ~~before in the past~~ has there been so many tornadoes.

nevertheless

Big word. Try the simpler words *but*, *still*, or *yet*.

new

Uncalled-for modifier when used with words that imply *new*.
It looked like a ~~new~~ beginning for everyone involved.
Bill set a ~~new~~ record in the decathlon.
They launched a website with new ~~and improved~~ features.

Other examples to consider include:

new baby	new discovery
new breakthrough	new initiative
new bride	new innovation
new change	new introduction
new construction	new invention
new creation	new neophyte
new departure	new recruit
new development	new revelation

no doubt that

Rambling. Pare this phrase to simply *doubtless* or *undoubtedly*.
~~No doubt that~~ undoubtedly their good name will be cleared.

no problem

A tired, overused phrase. Try *you're welcome* instead.
~~No problem.~~ You're welcome. Glad to help you.

no trespassing allowed (or permitted)

Verbal surplus. *Allowed* and *permitted* are unnecessary words.
We entered a no trespassing ~~allowed~~ area by accident.

nodded her (or his) head

Extra words. *Nodded* by itself will do.
The doctor watched as she nodded ~~her head~~ in response.

nomenclature terms

Repetition. Pick one of the two words.
The new release contains many new ~~nomenclature~~ terms.

nominal

Big word. Try the simpler words *slight* or *small*.

none at all

Wordy. At times, this phrase can be dropped.
No vacancies are available tonight~~, none at all~~.

nook and cranny

Repetition. Choose one or the other but not both.
We looked for it in every ~~nook and~~ cranny and found nothing.

(the) noon hour, (the) noontime

Overdone. Use the word *noon*.
Lunch will be formally served at ~~the~~ noon ~~hour~~.
The noon~~time~~ temperature is around 86 degrees Fahrenheit.

normal everyday

Word overkill. Often you can choose either adjective.
Cosmetic surgery is now part of ~~normal~~ everyday life.

(a) nostalgia for the past

Rambling. Just the word *nostalgia* will do.
We dwell more on ~~a~~ nostalgia ~~for the past~~ than the future.

not

The *not* word can lead to negative phrasing. Often a better word or phrase can be substituted.

~~Not many~~ few people follow his daily stock market advice.
For some reason, she is ~~not able~~ unable to access her account.
~~Not often~~ rarely do we see people here living beyond 90.

Other possibilities to consider include:

not accept – reject
not acceptable – unacceptable
not accurate – inaccurate
not actually true – untrue
not admit – deny
not allow – prevent
not certain – uncertain
not clearly – unclearly
not consider – ignore
not convicted – acquitted
not different – similar
not except – only if
not generous – cheap
not hardly – hardly
not have – lack
not honest – dishonest
not important – trivial
not in a position to – unable
not include – omit
not infrequently – often
not interested – uninterested
not later than – by
not old enough – too young
not on schedule – behind schedule
not on time – late
not possible – impossible
not the same – different
not unless – only if
not unlike – similar or alike
not until – only when
not very far from – relatively near
not withstanding the fact – although

not one single

Wordy. Delete the word *single*.
Not one ~~single~~ time did his predictions come true.

notable luminary

Redundant. *Luminaries* are *notable*.
A ~~notable~~ luminary presented the keynote speech today.

noted in the previous

Verbose. The phrase *noted earlier* is simpler.
As noted ~~in the previous section~~ earlier, bring proper ID.

notwithstanding the fact that

Long-winded. *Although*, *despite*, and *even though* are simpler.
Students may, ~~notwithstanding the fact that~~ despite section (1), apply.

now currently

Verbal surplus. At times, you can delete both words.
Her father is ~~now currently~~ the math department chair.

now pending

Word overkill. Choose one or the other but not both.
A bill~~,~~ ~~now~~ pending in the Senate~~,~~ gives aid to education.

(a) number of

Clutter. The word *many* can replace this phrase.
~~A number of~~ many people voiced their opposition.

number one leader

Unneeded modifier. Use the word *leader* alone.
Her company is the ~~number one~~ leader in solar power.

numerous

Bulky word. Try the word *many*.

O

"Writing became such a process of discovery that I couldn't wait to get to work in the morning: I wanted to know what I was going to say."—Sharon O'Brien

obfuscation
Big word. *Confused* or *perplexed* are simpler word choices.

objective
Big noun. Try *aim* or *goal*.

obligated
Inflated word. Try *bound*, *compelled*, or *required*.

obliterate
Hefty word. Try *cancel*, *destroy*, or *erase*.

(an) obsolete thing of the past
Long-winded. *Obsolete* is plenty.
Will audio cassettes become ~~an~~ obsolete ~~thing of the past~~?

obtained from
Chatty. Sometimes the word *of* can replace this phrase.
Samples ~~obtained from~~ of two lakes showed low toxic levels.

obviate
Bulky word. Try *avert*, *avoid*, or *prevent*.

obviously
Excess. Often this word can be cut.
It appears he ~~obviously~~ received the memo on dress code.

occasional irregularity
Unneeded modifier. Omit *occasional*.
The natural tea may work for ~~occasional~~ irregularity.

occupation

Big word. Try the simpler word *job*.

occur again

Rambling. Use the verb *recur*.
The next hybrid eclipse will not ~~occur again~~ recur until 2023.

occurrence

Bulky word. Go with the simpler word *event*.

oddly peculiar

Extra word. The adverb *oddly* is not needed.
We sensed something ~~oddly~~ peculiar concerning the request.

odorous smell

Redundant. All *smells* are *odorous*.
The new disinfectant will rid the house of the ~~odorous~~ smell.

of

Verbal surplus. A useless preposition often deleted.
They immediately took half ~~of~~ the profits from the sale.

of a

Chatty. A common phrase often leading to wordiness.
Her song writing genius was ~~of a most~~ peculiar ~~kind~~.
The problem with the virus software was ~~of a~~ strange ~~type~~.

Other examples to consider include:

of a bright color – bright
of a cheap quality – cheap
of a dangerous character – dangerous
of a high order – high
of a profitable character – profitable
of considerable magnitude – big, great

of all time

Word padding. A prepositional phrase often discarded.
Some regard Jimi Hendrix as the greatest guitarist ~~of all time~~.
"Citizen Kane" is her favorite film ~~of all time~~.

of minor importance

Empty phrase. The word *unimportant* is more condensed.
What occurred first is ~~of minor importance~~ unimportant.

of the

Transposing and using possessives can replace this phrase.
The operator of the machine vs. *The machine's operator.*

off

Off is often a needless ending preposition following a verb.
Instead of listing it, they will auction ~~off~~ their house.
How long will it take you to pay ~~off~~ your credit card balance?
The coupon lets us subtract another 10% ~~off~~.
If you get sap on your clothes, wash it ~~off~~ immediately.

Other possibilities to consider include:

better off	seal off
chop off	sent off
cut off	sever off
dust it off	shoot off
fight off	sold off
jump off	started off
kill it off	taper off
launched off	ticked off
rope off	wipe it off
save $10 off	

off in the distance

Extra word. The word *off* is sometimes not needed.
Suddenly we could hear a loud cry ~~off~~ in the distance.

off of

Wordy. Often you can drop the preposition *of*.
After their awards, the recipients stepped off ~~of~~ the stage.

offensive stench

Redundant. Any *stench* is *offensive*.
Hydrogen sulfide is a colorless gas with ~~an offensive~~ stench.

offer a recommendation, offer a solution, offer a suggestion

Long-winded. Use the verbs *recommend*, *solve*, or *suggest*.
We will ~~offer a recommendation~~ recommend they have a debate.
They may ~~offer a solution to~~ solve the overcrowding problem.
I will ~~offer a suggestion about~~ suggest an idea that works well.

offered resistance

Wordy. Use the verb *resisted*.
Many tenants ~~offered resistance~~ resisted the new regulations.

officiated at the ceremony

Unneeded ending phrase. *Officiated* by itself will do.
At June's graduation, Dr. Ward officiated ~~at the ceremony~~.

often times

Verbal surplus. The word *often* is plenty.
Often ~~times~~ we hear how television can influence people.

old

A redundant modifier in phrases where *old* is implied.
For years, the programmers used ~~an old~~ legacy system.

Other examples to consider include:

old adage	old maxim
old antique	old pioneer
old classic	old proverb
old cliché	old relic
old custom	old saying
old dowager	old tradition
old fossil	old veteran

on

Extra word. At times, this is a preposition we do not need.
The board of directors meets ~~on~~ every Wednesday morning.

on a daily basis

Verbose. Trim this phrase to the simple adverb *daily*.
The index measures consumer confidence ~~on a~~ daily ~~basis~~.

The same advice applies to these phrases:

on a monthly basis – monthly
on a periodic basis – periodically
on a weekly basis – weekly
on a yearly basis – yearly
on an hourly basis – hourly
on an individual basis – individually

on a few occasions

Muddle. Use the word *occasionally*.
~~On a few occasions~~ occasionally he explored political office.

on account of the fact that

Chatty. Use the words *as*, *because*, or *considering*.
He won ~~on account of the fact that~~ because he debated well.

on behalf of

Rambling. Say *for*.
She has worked hard ~~on behalf of~~ for many good causes.

on most occasions, on numerous occasions

Rambling. Use the words *usually* or *often*.
~~On most occasions~~ usually the classes are under two hours.
He has testified ~~on numerous occasions~~ often in court.

on the basis of

Verbose. *After*, *by*, and *from* can replace this phrase.
Prejudice ~~on the basis of~~ from such a disability is prohibited.

on the date of

Clutter. Use the preposition *on*.
Her birthday is on ~~the date of~~ our wedding anniversary.

on the grounds

Wordy. Try replacing this phrase with *because*.
She left ~~on the grounds~~ because of another opportunity.

on the occasion of

Rambling. At times, you can go with the word *on*.
On ~~the occasion of~~ our 20th anniversary, we went to Europe.

on the order of

Verbose. Try *almost*, *nearly*, or *roughly* to replace this phrase.
The company has ~~on the order of~~ nearly 1,000 employees.

on the part of

Chatty. *By* or *for* can sometimes replace this phrase.
The omission was an oversight ~~on the part of~~ by our staff.

on the scene

Muddle. At times, this phrase can be dropped.
Law enforcement should appear ~~on the scene~~ shortly.

on the subject of

Tedious. At times, the word *about* is a tighter replacement.
He testified ~~on the subject of~~ about insurance fraud.

on those occasions

Long-winded. This phrase can sometimes be removed.
~~On those occasions~~ when you know, report it immediately.

on two different occasions, on two separate occasions

Chatty. Say *twice*.
~~On two different occasions~~ twice she studied abroad.

one after another in succession

Rambling. The word *continuously* can replace this long phrase.
I hit golf balls continuously ~~one after another in succession~~.

one and only

Verbal surplus. Sometimes the phrase *and only* can be cut.
It's the one ~~and only~~ web site we visit for financial advice.

one and the same

Clutter. Use the phrase *the same*.
His story themes are ~~one and~~ the same in all his novels.

100 percent pure

Wordy. At times, the word *pure* can be omitted.
They claim their hamburgers are 100 percent ~~pure~~ beef.

one single person, one single reason, one single vote

Extra word. The adjective *single* is not needed.
The glider was designed for only one ~~single~~ person.
We can point to one ~~single~~ reason for poor sales last year.
She lost her local election by one ~~single~~ vote.

ongoing and continual

Repetition. Choose either *ongoing* or *continual*.
Training is an ongoing ~~and continual~~ part of our process.

ongoing work in progress

Excess. The word *ongoing* can be dropped.
Our process document is ~~an ongoing~~ work in progress.

(the) only difference being

Long-winded. The word *except* is crisper.
It's the same film ~~the only difference being~~ except it's edited.

open cavity, open forum, open trench

Verbal surplus. The word *open* is extra.
We found a large ~~open~~ cavity in an old tree.
The FTC's ~~open~~ forum on interest rates was a success.
An ~~open~~ trench unattended can be a safety hazard.

optimal, optimum

Plush words. Try *best* or *ideal* instead.

optimize and maximize

Redundant verbs. Choose one or the other but not both.
Advertising can optimize ~~and maximize~~ business success.

optional accessory

See entry for **additional accessory, optional accessory**.

optional choice (or extras)

Redundant. *Choices* and *extras* are *optional*.
The ~~optional~~ extras pictured are not in the base price.

opulent

Elegant word. *Lavish*, *rich*, or *wealthy* are simpler choices.

or alternatively

Needless ending word. Delete *alternatively*.
Follow the link below or ~~alternatively~~ click this button.

orbit around

Word overkill. The verb *orbit* alone is plenty.
The satellite will orbit ~~around~~ the earth next week.

order and direct

Repetition. Choose one or the other but not both.
We can order ~~and direct~~ them, but it's their option to comply.

organizationally structure

Overstated. The word *organizationally* can be cut.
We decided how to ~~organizationally~~ structure the program.

original founder, original source

Redundant. *Founder* and *source* assume being *original*.
He is the ~~original~~ founder and a key sponsor of the charity.
That novel was the ~~original~~ source for her winning screenplay.

originally

Needless modifier in phrases such as:

Many believe man was ~~originally~~ created in God's image.
Pop Warner Football was ~~originally~~ founded in 1929.

Other possibilities to consider include:

originally began
originally coined
originally conceived
originally debuted
originally discovered
originally established

originally introduced
originally invented
originally revealed
originally started
originally uncovered
originally unveiled

originate

Large word. The simpler words *begin* or *start* say the same thing.

ostentatious

Large word. *Brazen* or *showy* are simpler word choices.

other choices

Unessential modifier. Delete the word *other*.
She spoke on nutrition and the ~~other~~ choices for a healthy life.

out

Out is usually a needless preposition when following a verb.
These measurements extend ~~out~~ to satellites' altitudes.
The Internet company gave us tips on how to filter ~~out~~ spam.
Acting in films is one way of living ~~out~~ her dreams.
For your convenience, you can print ~~out~~ the manual as a PDF.
We were tired ~~out~~ from the long cross country trip.

Other possibilities to consider include:

balance out
beat out
block out
broadcast out
burst out
camp out
cancel out
check it out
clean out
clear out
contract out
crowd out
cut out
delete out
die out
dribble out
drown out
edit out
eliminate out
emerge out
empty out
excised out
exit out
extend out
extrapolate out
ferret out
fight it out
figuring out
find out
flatten out
flush out
found out
frozen out
hammer out
help out
hide out
lend out

lock out
lose out
map out
mellow out
miss out
net out
pay out
plan out
play out
plot out
precipitate out
protrude out
prune out
radiate out
raining out
rent out
root out
seek out
select out
send out
separate out
serve out
settle out
shut out
snowing out
sold out
sort it out
sought out
sound out
spell out
spit out
spread out
start out
stressed out
stretch out
strike it out
swap out

test out
trim it out
try out
type out
vent out
vetted out
watch out for
weeds out
win out
work it out
write out

outdoor picnic

Redundant. *Picnics* are *outdoors*.
They carry a large selection of folding ~~outdoor~~ picnic tables.

outside of

See entry for ***inside of***.

outside the realm of possibility

Rambling. Try *impossible*, *inconceivable*, or *unimaginable* instead.
It's ~~outside the realm of possibility~~ impossible that he is guilty.

outstanding loan, existing loan

Redundant. Loans are either *outstanding* or *existing*.
For once, they do not have any ~~outstanding~~ car loans.
Refinancing your ~~existing~~ loan will result in a lower rate.

outward

Awkward. Use the word *out*.
As the antennas are moved out~~ward~~, the signal gets worst.

over

In many cases, *over* is unnecessary when following a verb.
She came ~~over~~ here and immediately applied for citizenship.
Soon the company will convert ~~over~~ to a new billing system.
The high wall stopped the river from flooding ~~over~~ the park.
What group are you planning to invite ~~over~~ for the meeting?
When reading books, I typically skip ~~over~~ the front matter.
The housing slowdown may spill ~~over~~ into other areas.
It's now okay to switch ~~over~~ to the new operating system.

over and above

Muddle. The word *beyond* is more concise.
She went ~~over and above~~ beyond the client's requirements.

over and done

Overload. Either word will do.
Though a rewarding experience, I'm glad it's over ~~and done~~.

over and over

Repetitive. The adverb *repeatedly* says the same thing.
He kept saying the statement ~~over and over~~ repeatedly.

over exaggerate

Extra word. The modifier *over* is not needed.
They ~~over~~ exaggerate their benefits and compensation.

over the duration of, for the duration of

Verbose. Say *during*, *throughout*, or *while*.
Her car was used ~~over the duration of~~ during the TV show.

over with

Wordy. The preposition *with* can be removed.
We're looking forward to when the campaign is over ~~with~~.

overdone a little too much

Rambling. *Overdone* by itself is plenty.
The server agreed the meat was overdone ~~a little too much~~.

overseas international

The word *overseas* is surplus.
The product did well in all ~~overseas~~ international markets.

overused cliché

Redundant. All *clichés* are *overused*.
Presidential campaigns typically have ~~overused~~ clichés.

(an) overwhelming majority of the

Chatty. Say *most*.
~~An overwhelming majority of the~~ most people liked the offer.

owing to the fact that, owing to the reason that, owing to the situation that

Long-winded. Replace these phrases with the word *because*.
~~Owing to the fact that~~ because we were late, we were overlooked.

own personal opinion

Redundant. The phrase *own personal* is unnecessary.
What is your ~~own personal~~ opinion of the cell phone law?

P

"Put it before them briefly so they will read it, clearly so they will appreciate it, picturesquely so they will remember it and, above all, accurately so they will be guided by its light."—Joseph Pulitzer

paired in twos
Word overkill. Use the verb *paired*.
All the animals were paired in twos entering his ark.

palm of the hand
Verbal surplus. The word *palm* is sometimes all you need.
The magician held the hidden coin in the palm of the hand.

panacea for all ills
Excess. *For all ills* can often be deleted.
Some feel a vegetarian diet is the panacea for all ills.

paradigm
Jargon word. *Example*, *model*, or *pattern* are other choices.

participation and involvement
Redundant nouns. Choose one or the other but not both.
We encourage participation and involvement of all members.

particular interest
Overstated. The adjective *particular* can usually be cut.
If you have any particular interest, please let us know.

particular type of
Long-winded. Typically this filler phrase can be cut.
Any particular type of hotel you recommend is fine with us.

passed through a filter
Word padding. The word *filtered* is crisper.
For purification, the water is passed through a filter filtered.

passing fad, passing phase

Extra word. The modifier *passing* is not needed.
I predict blogging will be another ~~passing~~ Internet fad.
The economic slowdown is merely a ~~passing~~ phase.

past

A redundant modifier when the word *past* is already implied.
We know from ~~past~~ experience how important writing is.

Other examples to consider include:

past accomplishment	past overdue
past achievement	past performance
past deed	past precedents
past history	past record
past memory	past tradition

patently clear, patently obvious

Excess. The word *patently* is extra in both phrases.
The explanation must be ~~patently~~ clear to the audience.
Proper copyright conformity is not always ~~patently~~ obvious.

pathological disease

Redundant. *Diseases* are *pathological*.
Olive leafs help immune systems fight ~~pathological~~ disease.

pause for a moment

Verbal surplus. *Pause* by itself is fine.
Let's pause ~~for a moment~~ and thank those who helped us.

pending receipt of

Trite business letter phrase. Try to avoid it.

(a) percentage of the

Long-winded. Use the word *some*.
~~A percentage of the~~ some people never partake in the event.

perfect ideal, perfect utopia

Overstated. *Ideal* and *utopia* imply being *perfect*.
Many refer to him as the ~~perfect~~ ideal of generosity.
People have different ideas regarding a ~~perfect~~ utopia.

perfectly clear, perfectly legitimate

Excess. The adverb *perfectly* is not needed.
Today is the first ~~perfectly~~ clear day we've had in a month.
Spam filters sometimes catch ~~perfectly~~ legitimate messages.

perfidious

Complex word. *Deceitful, dishonest,* or *disloyal* are simpler
choices.

(a) period of

Excess. This phrase can usually be cut.
We will be gone for ~~a period of~~ five days next month.

permeate the entire, permeate throughout

Overstated. You can usually drop *entire* or *throughout*.
Garlic can permeate the ~~entire~~ house with an enticing aroma.
Her untiring enthusiasm permeates ~~throughout~~ the group.

permit the reduction of

Roundabout. The verb *reduce* is more direct.
This ~~permits the reduction of~~ reduces the deficit by next year.

perpetual

Big word. The simpler words *constant* and *forever* mean the
same.

persistent obsession

Redundant. Any *obsession* is *persistent*.
He has ~~a persistent~~ an obsession for moving overseas.

personal

Needless modifier for things already considered *personal*.
Check you didn't leave any ~~personal~~ belongings in the hotel.
They sincerely value your ~~personal~~ friendship.

Other possibilities to consider include:

personal belief	personal opinion
personal bias	personal point of view
personal charm	personal rapport
personal feelings	personal view
personal individual	

personally

Extra word. This word can often be deleted.
I ~~personally~~ reviewed the article.
I ~~personally~~ believe him.
I want to address them ~~personally~~.
~~Personally~~, it's a good idea.

pertaining to

Excess. The preposition *about* can replace this phrase.
The document ~~pertaining to~~ about his legal status was lost.

pervaded the whole, pervaded throughout

Overstated. The words *whole* and *throughout* can be dropped.
The flower's unique fragrance pervaded the ~~whole~~ garden.
Comedy and joy pervaded ~~throughout~~ the movie.

photosensitive to light

Redundant. *Photosensitive* implies *lighting*.
They found the gene that makes eyes photosensitive ~~to light~~.

physical appearance

Redundant. *Appearance* assumes something being *physical*.
Plastic surgery changed his entire ~~physical~~ appearance.

physically

Verbal surplus. At times, this word can be discarded.
The new car is not ~~physically~~ in the showroom.

pick and choose

Verbal glut. One of these words will do.
Deregulation lets us pick ~~and choose~~ the cable company.

pick your brain

Tired cliché that could be replaced by the phrase *get information or ideas*, etc.

piercing scream

Redundant. *Screams* are *piercing*.
A ~~piercing~~ scream could easily be heard in the distance.

pioneer breakthrough

Redundant. *Breakthroughs* and *pioneers* are similar.
The surgical method is a ~~pioneer~~ breakthrough in medicine.

(a) place where

Overstated. Sometimes the phrase *a place* can be cut.
That store is ~~a place~~ where one can find fresh organic foods.

place an order for, place its seal of approval on, place pressure on, place under arrest

Chatty. Use the verbs *order*, *approve*, *pressure*, or *arrest*.
They ~~placed an order for~~ ordered a new HDTV.
The FDA ~~placed its seal of approval on~~ approved a new drug.
Commodity prices ~~placed~~ pressured ~~on~~ all local prices.
The opposition leader was ~~placed under arrest~~ arrested again.

plain and simple

Overstated. Either word will do.
The secret of good writing is keeping it plain ~~and simple~~.

plan ahead, plan for the future, plan in advance, plan of action

Long-winded. The verb *plan* is typically enough.
Realistically, you must plan ~~ahead~~ if you want to retire early.
If I plan ~~for the future~~ correctly, I may avoid financial worries.
Please plan ~~in advance~~ to manage any emergency situation.
We followed her plan ~~of action~~ to develop better leaders.

please be advised, please do not hesitate to, please feel free to, please find enclosed

Business letter templates that need replacements.
~~Please be advised.~~ Be aware.
~~Please do not hesitate to contact us.~~ Please contact us.
~~Please feel free to.~~ Please.
~~Please find enclosed the estimate.~~ I'm enclosing the estimate.

pleased and contented, pleased and delighted

Redundant adjectives. Choose one or the other but not both.
We felt pleased ~~and contented~~ over the election results.
She was pleased ~~and delighted~~ to co-sign on his behalf.

p.m. in the evening

Overstated. *In the evening* is an unneeded phrase.
Showers are in effect from 9 p.m. ~~in the evening~~ to 3 a.m.

(the) point I am trying to make is that

Long-winded. At times, this hesitation device can be cut.
~~The point I am trying to make is that~~ opinions do matter.

poisonous venom

Redundant. Any *venom* is *poisonous*.
The scorpion uses its tail to deliver its ~~poisonous~~ venom.

polar opposite

Redundant. *Opposite* implies *polar*.
Libertarianism is the ~~polar~~ opposite of neo-conservatism.

polite euphemism

Redundant. By definition, *euphemisms* are *polite*.
Economically deprived is a ~~polite~~ euphemism for being poor.

popular consensus, popular myth

Redundant. A *consensus* and a *myth* have to be *popular*.
A ~~popular~~ consensus has HD satellite better than HD cable.
Many ~~popular~~ myths exists about the greenhouse effect.

positive benefits

Redundant. *Benefits* imply something *positive*.
Despite the dangers, sunlight also has ~~positive~~ benefits.

(the) possibility exists that

Verbose. At times, this phrase can be dropped.
~~The possibility exists that~~ you could have fiscal problems.

possibly may, possibly might

Extra modifiers. *May* and *might* both imply *possibility*.
The extra fees ~~possibly~~ may be off set by high returns.

postpone until later

Extra words. *Until later* is not needed.
We were told the meeting will be postponed ~~until later~~.

potential candidate, potential prospect, potential threat

Unneeded modifier. Omit the word *potential*.
The ~~potential~~ presidential candidate visited New Hampshire.
We face the ~~potential~~ prospect that free lunches may end.
The virus was a greater ~~potential~~ threat than we thought.

potentially capable, potentially may

Unneeded modifier. Delete the word *potentially*.
Penicillin is ~~potentially~~ capable of inducing allergic reactions.
This invention ~~potentially~~ may be developed jointly.

pragmatic

Complex word. *Practical*, *realistic*, or *sensible* are simpler choices.

precise and exact

Redundant adjectives. Choose one or the other but not both.
Unlike writing, math is a precise ~~and exact~~ subject.

precisely the same

Word overkill. The word *precisely* can be cut.
Bills pass the House and Senate in ~~precisely~~ the same form.

precocious

Large word. *Bright, gifted*, or *talented* are simpler word choices.

predicated on the assumption that

A roundabout way to say *assumed*.
It's ~~predicated on the assumption that~~ assumed people without health insurance will not seek medical care.

predicting future

Sometimes the word *future* is not needed.
Nostradamus was known for predicting ~~future~~ events.

predominant

Stuffy word. Try using *chief, main, major*, or *prime*.

pre-heat, pre-plan, pre-record

The *pre* is a needless prefix and modifier.
You first need to ~~pre-~~ heat the oven for 10 minutes.
If we ~~pre-~~plan correctly, we should have few surprises.
The game was ~~pre-~~ recorded three hours earlier.

prejudge in advance, prepare in advance

Redundant. *Prejudging* and *preparing* are always done *in advance*.
The jury was told not to prejudge ~~in advance~~ the defendant.
I will help you prepare ~~in advance~~ for the interview.

preliminary draft

Redundant. All *drafts* are in a *preliminary* stage.
We reviewed a ~~preliminary~~ draft proposal last week.

preordained destiny

Redundant. Any *destiny* is *preordained*.
Some believe we all have a ~~preordained~~ destiny from God.

preparation beforehand

Fatty phrase. Just go with the word *preparation*.
If you've done the preparation ~~beforehand~~, I see no problem.

prepay first

Overdone. Use *prepay* alone.
After 6 p.m., please prepay ~~first~~ before pumping fuel.

prescribed protocol

Redundant. *Protocol* is always *prescribed*.
Data should be recorded according to a ~~prescribed~~ protocol.

presence of

Overdone. Often this phrase can be removed.
The sample discloses ~~the presence of~~ high blood sugar.

present in greater abundance

Rambling. The phrase *more abundant* means the same.
Wealth is ~~present in greater abundance~~ more abundant here.

present incumbent

Redundant. An *incumbent* is associated with the *present*.
The ~~present~~ incumbent has no interest for a second term.

presently

Unneeded and misused word that technically means *in a short time* or *soon*, not *at this time* or *now*.
The board is meeting ~~presently~~ at the town hall.
She is ~~presently~~ studying three foreign languages in college.

pretty

Sometimes an excess qualifier. Delete.

She was always a ~~pretty~~ good scholar in all her coursework.

previous

Excess modifier in phrases implying something in the past.

His ~~previous~~ history of behavior may invite such suspicion.

Other examples to consider include:

previous accomplishment
previous achievement
previous deed
previous experience

previous to

Wordy. Often the word *before* is simpler.

~~Previous to~~ before arriving, little work was done on the plan.

previously existing, previously recorded

Overkill. *Existing* and *recorded* already imply *previously*.

He wrote the chapter using ~~previously~~ existing material.
The golf match was ~~previously~~ recorded three hours ago.

prior

Needless introductory word.

They have no ~~prior~~ history of late credit card payments.

Other possibilities to consider include:

prior approval
prior arrangement
prior blessing
prior consent
prior forecast
prior notice

prior planning
prior precedent
prior precursor
prior preparation
prior reservation
prior scouting

prioritization

Pompous word. Use the word *ranking*.

proceed ahead, proceed forth, proceed forward, proceed further, proceed onward

Excess. *Proceed* alone will do in all these cases.
We are going to proceed ~~ahead~~ with every recommendation.
It's the patient's choice to proceed ~~forth~~ with elective surgery.
After entering the gate, proceed ~~forward~~ to River Street.
Before we proceed ~~further,~~ other issues need addressing.
You can proceed ~~onward~~ until you reach the intersection.

process

Unneeded word. Often this noun can be deleted.
The much needed healing ~~process~~ began last week.
For many students, vocabulary is ~~an~~ on-going ~~process~~.

procrastinate

Large word. *Defer, delay*, or *postpone* are simpler word choices.

productively useful

Redundant. If you're *productive*, you're also *useful*.
Working together will make them more ~~productively~~ useful.

proficiency

Inflated word. The word *skill* means the same.

profusion

Stuffy word. The words *glut* or *plenty* are simpler.

progress forward

Chatty. The verb *progress* is plenty.
The chairperson let us progress ~~forward~~ on the issue.

project ahead, forecast ahead

Needless repeating of the same idea. Omit *ahead*.
The music company will project ~~ahead~~ this year's releases.
He tried to forecast ~~ahead~~ the company's year-end revenue.

projected forecast
Redundant. All *forecasts* are *projected*.
Readership has exceeded our ~~projected~~ forecast of 60,000.

proliferate
Complex word. *Grow*, *increase*, or *spread* are simpler words.

prolong the duration of
Wordy. The verb *prolong* is sometimes a shorter substitute.
The medicine did not prolong ~~the duration of~~ my cold.

promptly and right away
Word overkill. Use the adverb *promptly*.
Make sure you see your doctor promptly ~~and right away~~.

promulgate
Big word. *Advertise*, *announce*, *issue*, or *publish* are simpler words.

(a) proportion of the
The word *some* can replace this phrase.
We donated ~~a proportion of the~~ some profits to local charities.

proposed plan
Redundant. All *plans* are *proposed*.
The board adopted our ~~proposed~~ plan for a new town hall.

prosaic
Formal word. *Dull* or *ordinary* are simpler words.

proselytize
Complex word for *convert*.

protective armor, protective helmet
Excess modifiers. *Armor* and *helmets* are *protective*.
The ~~protective~~ armor contains penetration-resistant fabric.
~~Protective~~ helmets can prevent head and brain injuries.

protest against

Verbal surplus. The verb *protest* is plenty.
The workers will likely protest ~~against~~ the job regulations.

prototype model

Redundant. A *prototype* is a *model*.
Her prototype ~~model~~ set the new standard in engineering.

prove conclusively

Unneeded adverb. If you *prove* something, it is *conclusive*.
The attorney will prove ~~conclusively~~ Joe's innocence.

proven facts

Redundant. All *facts* are *proven*.
It's a ~~proven~~ fact global warming can melt the ice caps.

provide an estimate

Rambling. Try using the verb *estimate* as a replacement.
An appraiser will ~~provide an estimate~~ estimate the damages.

provide assistance

Wordy. The verb *help* can replace this phrase.
The law ~~provides assistance~~ helps those with disabilities.

provided

Extra word. Often this word can be removed.
The data ~~provided~~ in the leaflet is critical to the installation.

provided that

Chatty. Often the word *if* can replace this phrase.
~~Provided that~~ if you comply, you will certainly see a benefit.

provocative

Stuffy word. *Aggressive, insulting*, or *offensive* are simpler.

public forum, public notoriety

Redundant modifiers. *Forum* and *notoriety* imply the *public*.
The FTC held a ~~public~~ forum to discuss many issues.
From her successful work, she gained ~~public~~ notoriety.

purchase

Large word. Prefer the simpler verb *buy*.

pure and unadulterated

Redundant adjectives. Either word will do.
They found not all organic milk is pure ~~and unadulterated~~.

pure virgin

Redundant. *Virgin* implies *pure*.
The old well contained pure ~~virgin~~ spring water.

(the) purpose of

Word padding. A dull phrase often dropped.
The charity is for ~~the purpose of~~ helping the disadvantaged.

pursuant to your request

See entry for **in accordance with your request, in compliance with your request**.

pursue after

Overstated. The word *after* is not needed.
Next, she wished to pursue ~~after~~ her doctorate degree.

put across

Wordy. The word *explain* can replace this phrase.
Try to explain ~~put across~~ your position on the referendum.

put an end to

Long-winded. Use the verb *end*.
They launched a new website to ~~put an~~ end ~~to~~ global famine.

put in an appearance

Rambling. Use the verb *appear*.

My boss asked me to ~~put in an appearance~~ appear next week.

put off until later

Verbal surplus. Delete the phrase *until later*.

They put off ~~until later~~ nominating any candidates.

puzzling in nature

Overstated. The word *puzzling* is plenty.

The idea was puzzling ~~in nature~~ to us all.

Q

"Verbosity leads to unclear, inarticulate things."—Dan Quayle

qualified expert
Redundant. *Experts* must be *qualified*.
Some ~~qualified~~ experts do not recognize the new drug.

quantity of
Word padding. Sometimes this phrase can be discarded.
She still has ~~a~~ sufficient ~~quantity of~~ credits to graduate in May.

querulous
Complex word. *Difficult, grouchy,* or *irritable* are simpler choices.

(the) question as to whether
Dense. Use the word *whether*.
~~The question as to~~ whether it will happen is unknown.

questions and concerns
Overstated. One of these words will usually do.
Shareholders have questions ~~and concerns~~ over the merger.

quick dash
Redundant. A *dash* is usually *quick*.
After passing customs, it was a ~~quick~~ dash to the plane.

quickly expedite, speedily expedite
Needless adverbs. Use the word *expedite* by itself.
They wanted to ~~quickly~~ expedite the signing of the treaty.
We need to ~~speedily~~ expedite our passport application.

quite

Excess qualifier. Delete when possible.

The researchers are ~~quite~~ precise with all their data.

John's process was ~~quite~~ innovative and useful to all.

quite a few

Long-winded. Replace with the word *many*.

Her latest film makes ~~quite a few~~ many political innuendoes.

R

"Writing energy is like anything else: the more you put in, the more you get out."—Richard Reeves

raced quickly, dashed quickly
Redundant. Any *race* or *dash* is done *quickly*.
Both attorneys raced ~~quickly~~ through their summations.
Hope for a reconciliation between them was dashed ~~quickly~~.

rain precipitation, snow precipitation
Obvious redundancies.
The rain ~~precipitation~~ sensor uses common radar technology.
He noted the snow ~~precipitation~~, humidity, and temperature.

raining outside
*See entry for **hailing outside, snowing outside**.*

raise an objection
Muddle. Uncover the smothered verb, *object*.
The attorney will ~~raise an objection~~ object to any disclosure.

rancorous
Large word. *Bitter, ruthless*, or *unforgiving* are simpler word choices.

random chance
Redundant. Any *chance* is *random*.
Winning a lottery will always be a ~~random~~ chance.

ranges all the way from
Overstated. The phrase *range from* means the same.
The experience ranges ~~all the way~~ from 1 to 20 years.

rare albino

Redundant. *Albinos* are always *rare*.
The zoo houses many ~~rare~~ albino deer and squirrels.

rarely ever

Excess. Omit the word *ever*.
Access to their network drives is rarely ~~ever~~ granted.

(a) rate of

Wordy. At times, this phrase can be cut.
This year's enrollment grew at ~~a rate of~~ five students per class.

rate of speed

Try the word *rate* alone.
At her rate ~~of speed~~, she may set a racing record today.

rather

This excess qualifier and intensifier seldom adds anything.
Ben is ~~rather~~ well-known for his technical expertise.

rationale

Fancy word. The words *basis*, *grounds*, or *reasons* are simpler.

reach a conclusion

Overstated. The verb *conclude* can replace this phrase.
The panel may not ~~reach a conclusion~~ conclude today.

readily apparent

Word overkill. The word *readily* can be dropped.
The evidence for abrupt climate change is ~~readily~~ apparent.

real actual, real danger, real fact, real truth

The word *real* is surplus in all these phrases.
They may have discovered the ~~real~~ actual cure for colds.
Some over-the-counter drugs pose a ~~real~~ danger.
The investigator is still trying to uncover the ~~real~~ facts.
Her new book covers the ~~real~~ truth on melting ice caps.

realize a savings of

Verbose. Say *save*.
The coupons let us ~~realize a savings of~~ save more than $10.

realized from

Wordy. Sometimes the preposition *of* can replace this phrase.
Our funds are better than those ~~realized from~~ of last year.

really

This overused modifier adds little in phrases such as: *really dangerous*, *really essential*, *really excellent*, and *really horrible*.
Not all sharks are considered ~~really~~ dangerous to swimmers.
Is it ~~really~~ essential to bring a driver's license for identification?
The seminars at this year's conference were ~~really~~ excellent.
While under anesthesia, I had some ~~really~~ horrible dreams.

reason is because

Weak. Avoid this phrase by using the word *because*.
*The **reason** she didn't come **is because** she lost her ticket.*
vs.
She didn't come <u>because</u> she lost her ticket.

recapitulate

Elegant word. *Recap* or *repeat* are simpler choices.

reconciliation

Elegant word. *Compromise, reunion*, or *settlement* are simpler choices.

recorded history

Redundant. If it's *history*, a *record* exists.
This article discusses the ~~recorded~~ history of rock and roll.

recur over and over

Repetition. *Over and over* is unnecessary.
Typically her cold sores recur ~~over and over~~ in the winter.

recurring motif, recurring pattern

Chatty. The word *recurring* is unessential.

Cameos by Hitchcock were a ~~recurring~~ motif in his films.
The ~~recurring~~ pattern of late deliveries seems unlikely.

recycled and used again

Repetition. *Recycled* alone is plenty.

The dirty oil can be recycled ~~and used again~~.

reduce the speed of

Excess. This phrase can often be trimmed to *slow*.

Simple drag can ~~reduce the speed of~~ slow many objects.

redundant abbreviations

Often the word following an abbreviation is not needed because it is part of the abbreviation. This is sometimes referred to as RAP (Redundant Acronym Phrase) or RAS (Redundant Acronym Syndrome).

Some popular examples include:

ABS system – ABS means *Antilock Braking System.*
AC current – AC means *Alternating Current.*
ADD disorder – ADD means *Attention Deficit Disorder.*
AFC conference – AFC means *American Football Conference.*
AIDS syndrome – AIDS means *Acquired Immune Deficiency Syndrome.*
AM modulation – AM means *Amplitude Modulation.*
APR rate – APR means *Annual Percentage Rate.*
ARM mortgage – ARM means *Adjustable Rate Mortgage.*
ATM machine – ATM means *Automated Teller Machine.*
CAD design – CAD means *Computer-Assisted Design.*
CGA adapter – CGA means *Color Graphics Adapter.*
CNN network – CNN means *Cable News Network.*
CPI index – CPI means *Consumer Price Index.*
CPU unit – CPU means *Central Processing Unit.*
CRT tube – CRT means *Cathode Ray Tube.*
DAT tape – DAT means *Digital Audio Tape.*
DC current – DC means *Direct Current.*
DOS system – DOS means *Disk Operating System.*

DSL line – DSL means *Digital Subscriber Line*.

DVD disc – DVD means *Digital Video* (or *Versatile*) *Disc*.

EBCDIC code – EBCDIC means *Extended Binary Coded Decimal Interchange Code*.

EST time – EST means *Eastern Standard Time*.

ETA arrival – ETA means *Estimated Time of Arrival*.

FM modulation – FM means *Frequency Modulation*.

GIF format – GIF means *Graphic Interchange Format*.

GMT time – GMT means *Greenwich Mean Time*.

GOP party – GOP means *Grand Old Party*.

GPS system – GPS means *Global Positioning System*.

HIV virus – HIV means *Human Immunodeficiency Virus*.

HTML language – HTML means *HyperText Markup Language*.

ICU unit – ICU means *Intensive Care Unit*.

IPO offering – IPO means *Initial Program Offering*.

IRA account – IRA means *Individual Retirement Account*.

ISBN number – ISBN means *International Standard Book Number*.

ISDN network – ISDN means *Integrated Services Digital Network*.

KFC chicken – KFC means *Kentucky Fried Chicken*.

LAN network – LAN means *Local Area Network.*

LCD display – LCD means *Liquid Crystal Display*.

LED diode – LED means *Light Emitting Diode*.

MIDI interface – MIDI means *Musical Instrument Digital Interface*.

MST time – MST means *Mountain Standard Time*.

NATO organization – NATO means *North Atlantic Treaty Organization*.

NFC conference – NFC means *National Football Conference*.

NPR radio – NPR means *National Public Radio*.

OPEC countries – OPEC means *Organization of the Petroleum Exporting Countries*.

PDF format – PDF means *Portable Document Format*.

PIN number – PIN means *Personal Identification Number*.

PST time – PST means *Pacific Standard Time*.

RAM memory – RAM means *Random Access Memory*.

ROM memory – ROM means *Read Only Memory*.

SALT talks – SALT means *Strategic Arms Limitations Talks*.

SAM missile – SAM means *Surface-to-Air Missile*.

SPF factor – SPF means *Skin Protection Factor*.

START treaty – START means *Strategic Arms Reduction Treaty*.

SUV vehicle – SUV means *Sport Utility Vehicle*.

UHF frequency – UHF means *Ultra-High Frequency*.
UL laboratories – UL means *Underwriters Laboratories*.
UN nations – UN means *United Nations*.
UPC code – UPC means *Universal Product Code*.
UPI international – UPI means *United Press International*.
VAT tax – VAT means *Value Added Tax*.
VHF frequency – VHF means *Very High Frequency*.
VIN number - VIN means *Vehicle Identification Number*.

re-elected for another term

Overstated. The word *re-elected* will do.
Mary was re-elected ~~for another term~~ on the town board.

referred to as

Word overkill. Use the words *called* or *known as*.
Normal vision is typically ~~referred to as~~ called 20/20.

refrain from

Long-winded. Use the phrase *do not*.
Please ~~refrain from~~ do not leav~~ing~~ the meeting early.

regarding the matter of, concerning the matter of

Verbose. Use the word *about*.
More data ~~regarding the matter of~~ about the company is online.
My point ~~concerning the matter of~~ about him is unchanged.

regardless of the fact that

Word padding. At times, *although* and *even though* are more concise.
~~Regardless of the fact that~~ although you have strong convictions, your opinion is in the minority.

regular monthly meetings

Word overkill. Use the phrase *monthly meetings*.
We hold ~~regular~~ monthly meetings for your convenience.

regular routine

Unneeded modifier. A *routine* is something *regular*.
We try to inject exercise into our ~~regular~~ daily routine.

reimburse

Large word. Try the simpler word *repay*.

relatively precise

Precise does not carry any qualifier.
The exam will test a ~~relatively~~ precise range of writing skills.

relic from the past

Redundant. A *relic* is *from the past*.
Is that still a useful tool or a relic ~~from the past~~?

remainder

Large word. The word *rest* is a simpler word choice.

remaining remnant, remaining residue, remaining vestige

Extra word. The word *remaining* is not necessary.
We're trying to protect ~~remaining~~ remnants of that famous era.
The ~~remaining~~ residue consists of fluorine and oxygen.
This structure is the only ~~remaining~~ vestige of the building.

remains still

Clutter. Use the verb *remains*.
Oddly, the question of rights remains ~~still~~ unanswered.

reminisce about the past

Redundant. If you *reminisce*, it is about the *past*.
He met to renew friendships and reminisce ~~about the past~~.

remittance

Large word. Try the simpler word *payment*.

remove and eliminate

Redundant verbs. Go with the simpler word *remove*.
The liquid permanently removes ~~and eliminates~~ stains.

remuneration
Big word. Try the simpler words *pay*, *salary,* or *wages*.

render assistance to
Hefty phrase for the simple word *help*.
Could you ~~render assistance to~~ help with the cleanup?

repeat the same
Overstated. The verb *repeat* by itself will do.
It's possible, they could repeat ~~the same~~ mistakes.

required prerequisite
Unneeded modifier. Delete the word *required*.
Eve cannot register without the ~~required~~ prerequisites.

requirement
Complex word. Try *need* instead.

reservation
Large word. Try the simpler word *doubt*.

reserve ahead
Repetition. Delete the word *ahead*.
Hotels are often booked early, so reserve ~~ahead~~ now.

residual trace
Word overkill. *Residual* and *trace* are close in meaning.
A ~~residual~~ trace of material may be contaminated.

resultant effect
Overstated. The word *resultant* is not needed.
The ~~resultant~~ effect was a jump in energy demand.

results achieved so far
Excess. Omit the phrase *so far*.
The results achieved ~~so far~~ show the program is a success.

results in intensifying
Chatty. Use the verb *intensify*.
His words ~~results in intensifying~~ intensify his attack on him.

(the) results of
Often a needless phrase.
~~The results of~~ our findings support her original theory.

reveal for the first time
Needless ending phrase.
The magician reveals ~~for the first time~~ how she did it.

review and comment on
Double verbs. Choose one or the other.
Please review ~~and comment on~~ our new ethics policy.

rich opulence
Redundant. *Opulence* implies something *rich* or wealthy.
Deep burgundy can lend ~~rich~~ opulence to your decorating.

ridiculous nonsense
Overstated. The word *ridiculous* is not needed.
The paper never publishes such ~~ridiculous~~ nonsense.

right and proper
Redundant adjectives. Choose one or the other but not both.
In a sales letter, it's essential to get things right ~~and proper~~.

right-hand, right-hand side
Verbal surplus. The word *hand* is unnecessary.
You'll need to take a right ~~hand~~ turn at the next light.
Make comments on the right ~~hand~~ side of the page.

right now
Excess. Sometimes the word *right* can be discarded.
Here are a few things to do ~~right~~ now for your career.

rigorous

Big word. Try the simpler words *exact*, *harsh*, *strict*, or *thorough*.

root cause

Word overkill. The word *root* can be cut.
Overheating was the ~~root~~ cause of the computer problem.

rough estimate, rough guess, rough rule of thumb, rough sketch

The word *rough* is surplus in all these phrases.
He gave us ~~a rough~~ an estimate on remodeling the house.
We did a ~~rough~~ guess on how many would attend the class.
A ~~rough~~ rule of thumb defines a work month as 22 days.
Their tool can covert a ~~rough~~ sketch into a finished drawing.

round circle, round cylinder, round wheel

Unneeded modifier. All three objects assume a *round* shape.

round in shape

Extra words. The phrase *in shape* is filler.
The X-ray showed the fracture to be round ~~in shape~~.

rules and regulations

Overstated. One of these words will do.
We reserve the right to revise the rules ~~and regulations~~.

ruling junta

Chatty. *Junta* alone will do.
They asked the ~~ruling~~ junta to release certain prisoners.

rural or rustic country (farm)

Redundant. *Country* and *farms* are both *rural* and *rustic*.
They bought a ~~rural~~ country farm in update New Jersey.
We are in the market for a rustic ~~country~~ house

S

"It behooves us to avoid archaisms. Never use a long word when a diminutive one will do."—William Safire

safe haven, safe sanctuary
Redundant. *Havens* and *sanctuaries* are always safe.
Investors are looking for a ~~safe~~ haven from the recession.
They created a ~~safe~~ sanctuary for endangered animals.

sagacity
Prudence, shrewdness, or *wisdom* are simpler word choices.

same exact, same identical
Extra modifiers. Use the words *same, exact*, or *identical*.
I have the same ~~exact~~ networking problem as you do.
I have the ~~same~~ exact cell phone as you do.
It's the ~~same~~ identical test used in standard analysis.

sanguineous
The word *wise* is more common and precise.

saturate
The verbs *drench, flood*, or *soak* are simpler word choices.

save and except
Verbal surplus. Either word will do.
We sell everything, ~~save and~~ except small appliances.

scary nightmare
Redundant. All *nightmares* are *scary*.
If I watch that film, I'll probably have a ~~scary~~ nightmare.

scheduled appointment
Redundant. All *appointments* are *scheduled*.
If you can't make your ~~scheduled~~ appointment, please call.

screech noisily

Redundant. It's assumed a *screech* is *noisy*.
The metal chairs screech ~~noisily~~ on the concrete floors.

scribbled hurriedly

See entry for **hurriedly scribbled**.

scrutinize carefully, scrutinize in detail

Word overkill. *Scrutinize* alone is plenty.
The company will scrutinize ~~carefully~~ all job applicants.
The auditor scrutinizes ~~in detail~~ all expense accounts.

scurried rapidly

Word overkill. The word *rapidly* can be dropped.
The animal scurried ~~rapidly~~ toward an adjacent hollow log.

seasoned veteran

Redundant. A *veteran* is someone who is *seasoned*.
The firm needs a ~~seasoned~~ veteran to be a mentor.

secretly concealing

Redundant. When it's a *secret*, it should be *concealed*.
We noticed the magician ~~secretly~~ concealing many cards.

sedulous

Large word. Try the simpler word *busy*.

seedling plant

Redundant. A *plant* is a *seedling*.
The unexpected heavy frost killed the seedling ~~plant~~.

seems apparent

Excess. The word *apparent* isn't always needed.
It seems ~~apparent~~ your desire to be a doctor has changed.

seesaw up and down

Overstated. The phrase *up and down* is unnecessary.
Expect your career to seesaw ~~up and down~~ occasionally.

select and choose
Double verbs. One of these words will do.
My counselor helped me select ~~and choose~~ the right college.

selectively identify
Word overkill. The word *selectively* can be deleted.
She found a way to ~~selectively~~ identify all the bad cells.

self confessed
Overstated. The word *self* often is omitted.
When it's about studying, he's a ~~self~~ confessed bookworm.

self portrait of me
Repetition. Delete the phrase *of me*.
I had a self portrait ~~of me~~ done right after I turned 50.

send an invitation to
Rambling. The simple verb *invite* is shorter.
Please ensure you ~~send an invitation to~~ invite everyone.

separate and discrete, separate and distinct
Repetition. Choose one or the other but not both.
We prefer the two groups to remain ~~separate and~~ discrete.
A service renewal is a separate ~~and distinct~~ contract.

separate entity, separate individual
Unneeded modifiers. Delete the word *separate*.
The banks are not ~~separate~~ entities, only partnerships.
The book describes a bond between two ~~separate~~ individuals.

separate them apart
See entry for **crumble apart, split apart**.

serious crisis, serious danger
Redundant. *Crisis* and *danger* are always *serious*.
Budget issues put the athletic program in a ~~serious~~ crisis.
During the storm, they were definitely in ~~serious~~ danger.

seriously consider

Word overkill. If you're *considering*, you're probably *serious*.
Which candidate will you ~~seriously~~ consider voting for?

shapes and forms

Verbal excess. Either word will do.
New products come in many basic shapes ~~and forms~~.

share in common

Wordy. The phrase *in common* is not needed.
We share ~~in common~~ many basic and strong beliefs.

shared consensus, shared dialogue, shared partnership

Word overkill. The word *shared* is assumed in all these phrases.
We require there be a ~~shared~~ consensus about the rules.
We promote a ~~shared~~ dialogue among the faculty.
We recognize a ~~shared~~ partnership among the companies.

sharp point, sharp pungent, sharp thorn

Overstated. These objects are known to be *sharp*.

she herself

*See entry for **he himself**.*

short blurb

Redundant. A *blurb* is something *short*.
Write a ~~short~~ blurb stating your intentions for the society.

short overview, short summary, short synopsis

Overstated. All these words imply something being *short*.
Today he's giving a(n) ~~short~~ overview to the class.
She needs to give a ~~short~~ summary to the customers.
The report is intended as a ~~short~~ synopsis of the novel.

shorter in height, shorter in length, shorter in stature

Excess. The phrases *in height*, *in length*, and *in stature* are not needed.

The freshman football team is shorter ~~in height~~ this year.

The tension strips are shorter ~~in length~~ and will not buckle.

He developed a bike specifically for those shorter ~~in stature~~.

should a situation arise where

Long-winded. The word *if* is more concise.

~~Should a situation arise where~~ if you need help, please call.

should it prove to be

Tedious. The phrase *if that* could replace this long phrase.

~~Should it prove to be~~ if that's true, we have little recourse.

should you have any further questions

Overused business phrase. Prefer using: *But if you have any questions….*

shows a listing of

Wordy. The word *shows* by itself is often simpler.

The program shows ~~a listing of~~ the graduates and awards.

shrug one's shoulders

Extra word. Omit the word *shoulder*.

After hearing her story, we simply shrugged ~~our shoulders~~.

shuttle back and forth

Overstated. Delete the phrase *back and forth*.

They shuttle ~~back and forth~~ between Boston and New York.

sick leave time

Excess. The word *time* is not needed.

We may use accumulated sick leave ~~time~~ for other things.

significant major changes

Overstated. The word *significant* can be cut.
Route 17 needs ~~significant~~ major changes to the pavement.

significant proportion of

Verbose. The word *much* can replace this phrase.
~~A significant proportion of~~ much protein is in fish and milk.

similar to

Overstated. The word *like* means the same.
A drug ~~similar to~~ like Botox could help writer's cramp.

since the time of, since the time when

Wordy. The phrases *time of* and *the time when* can be omitted.
The music has changed much since the ~~time of~~ Beatles.
The flights are cheaper since ~~the time when~~ we flew last.

sincere and earnest

Overstated. One of these words will do.
They are sincere ~~and earnest~~ in stating their opposition.

single bachelor, single entity, single most, single one

Word overkill. The word *single* is unnecessary.
A one-room penthouse is available for a ~~single~~ bachelor.
In the eyes of the law, a corporation is a(n) ~~single~~ entity.
What is today's ~~single~~ most important piece of legislation?
Every ~~single~~ one of those effects was produced digitally.

sink to the bottom

Chatty. The word *sink* will do.
If we add more cargo, the boat may sink ~~to the bottom~~.

(a) situation in which

Verbose. Shorten this phrase to the word *when*.
Imagine ~~a situation in which~~ when a vote didn't count.

sizeable percentage of

Chatty. Say *many* or *most* instead.
A sizeable percentage of most songs are copyrighted.

skim quickly

Unneeded adverb. Use the verb *skim*.
Skim *quickly* the passage again before taking the test.

skip over

Word overkill. The word *over* is not always needed.
The professor felt we could skip *over* the next chapter.

skirt around

Unneeded ending word. Drop the word *around*.
They continually skirt *around* the real issues of the day.

slight trace

Redundant. Every *trace* is *slight*.
The fires left only a *slight* trace of smoke in the air.

slow speed

Excess. Use the word *slow* instead.
He led police on a slow *speed* chase through the city.

small

Needless modifier when the word *small* is already implied.
We live in a *small* hamlet in the New Hampshire mountains.
They found a *small* trace of alcohol in his bloodstream.

Other examples to consider include:

small bit	small in stature
small detail	small minority
small duckling	small morsel
small dwarf	small particle
small fraction	small sapling
small fragment	small shred
small hint	small smidgen
small infant	small speck
small iota	

small in size
The category of size is implied. Delete *in size*.
From the MRI, the tumor appeared small ~~in size~~.

(a) small number of
Verbose. The word *few* is crisper.
~~A small number of~~ few students applied for the scholarship.

smaller sized
Overstated. The adjective *smaller* is plenty by itself.
Joe has a smaller ~~sized~~ 21 speed mountain bike for sale.

smile on her (or his) face
Rambling. The noun *smile* by itself will do.
With a smile ~~on her face~~, she graciously accepted the award.

smuggled illegally
Redundant. If something is *smuggled*, it's done *illegally*.
The two rare birds were smuggled ~~illegally~~ into the country.

snow precipitation
*See entry for **rain precipitation**.*

snowing outside
*See entry for **hailing outside, raining outside***

so as to
Word padding. The word *to* is enough.
We researched six companies ~~so as~~ to get the best price.

so consequently, so therefore
Lengthy. The word *so* is plenty.
They are renovating the hotel so ~~consequently~~ it is closed.
We covered the topic, so ~~therefore~~ we need to move on.

so long as
*See entry for **as long as**.*

soaked to the skin

Word padding. Go just with the verb *soaked*.
After a few minutes of rain, they were soaked ~~to the skin~~.

sole and exclusive

Repetition. Choose one or the other but not both.
She has the sole ~~and exclusive~~ right to the early recordings.

sole of the foot

Word padding. The word *sole* is plenty.
The sole ~~of the foot~~ has thick, hairless skin.

some but not all, many but not all

Overstated. Use *some* or *many* instead.
The new spam filter rejects some ~~but not all~~ emails.
Many ~~but not all~~ tellers are sold on a new banking system.

some kind of

Verbal surplus. Delete this phrase.
Without ~~some kind of~~ extra help, we'll miss the deadline.

some of the

Wordy. Use the word *some*.
Some ~~of the~~ new toys can help your child's motor skills.

some time to come

Extra words. Drop the phrase *to come*.
Her company will be profitable for some time ~~to come~~.

somewhere in the neighborhood of

Long-winded. The words *about*, *almost*, or *nearly are* shorter.
It takes ~~somewhere in the neighborhood of~~ about an hour.

sort of

Excess. A phrase we can usually omit.
If elected, he will be a more proactive ~~sort of~~ city mayor.

(the) space of

Tedious. Sometimes this phrase can be dropped.
We wrote quality proposals in ~~the space of~~ two weeks.

specific details, specific example

Redundant modifiers. *Details* and *examples* are specific.
She is supplying ~~specific~~ details about the program.
Please give me ~~specific~~ examples of what you mean.

speedily expedite

*See entry for **quickly expedite**.*

spin in circles

Wordy. The verb *spin* is sometimes all you need.
Some dogs tend to spin ~~in circles~~ before they sit.

split apart

*See entry for **crumble apart, separate them apart**.*

(the) spring season

Redundant. It's implied *spring* is a *season*.
We always look forward to golf in ~~the~~ spring ~~season~~.

spur of the moment impulse

Word overkill. Use the noun *impulse*.
On ~~a spur of the moment~~ an impulse, we left for a vacation.

spur on

Excess. Omit the ending preposition *on*.
The thought of bonuses will spur them ~~on~~ to finish the task.

spurious

Inflated word. *Bogus, fake, false*, or *untrue* are simpler words.

square miles of area

Excess. *Of area* is a needless phrase.
The Pacific Ocean has 6,420,0000 square miles ~~of area~~.

standard custom
Unneeded modifier. *Customs* are *standard*.
Prayers before each meal is their ~~standard~~ custom.

state and express
Redundant verbs. Pick one.
State ~~and express~~ your concerns now before it's too late.

(the) state of
Extra words. Delete the phrase *the state of*.
She found the unique plant years ago in ~~the state of~~ Maine.

still continue, still linger, still pending, still persist, still remain
Excess. The word *still* adds nothing to these phrases.
The inflation rate ~~still~~ continues to be a government concern.
Despite the stock market rise, recession ~~still~~ lingers.
The new government contract award is ~~still~~ pending.
If the problem ~~still~~ persists, contact your cable company.
A cure for her cancer is a hope that ~~still~~ remains.

still standing today
Excess. The noun *today* can be removed.
The buildings built in the 1800s are still standing ~~today~~.

strange type of
Overstated. Often you can go with just the word *strange*.
They use a strange ~~type of~~ language among themselves.

strategize
Inflated verb. *Direct* or *plan* are much simpler verbs.

stress the point that
Verbal surplus. At times, the phrase *the point that* is unnecessary.
We stress ~~the point that~~ a tired staff hurts productivity.

strict disciplinarian

Redundant. All *disciplinarians* are *strict*.
He was known as a stern teacher and a ~~strict~~ disciplinarian.

strong and powerful

Redundant adjectives. Choose one or the other but not both.
We have a ~~strong and~~ powerful bond with the district.

strong commitment, strong conviction, strong resolution

Redundant. These things are assumed to be *strong*.
We have a ~~strong~~ commitment to our allies around the world.
If elected, he has a ~~strong~~ conviction to change the tax laws.
They made a ~~strong~~ resolution to quit smoking next year.

stumble accidentally

Redundant. Any time you *stumble*, it's an *accident*.
It's easy to stumble ~~accidentally~~ into unwanted websites.

stunted in growth

Word padding. The phrase *in growth* is implied here.
Thanks to the frost, the plants remain stunted ~~in growth~~.

subject matter

Chatty. Sometimes the word *matter* is irrelevant.
We browsed the huge database of courses by subject ~~matter~~.

submerged under water

Word padding. The word *submerged* is plenty.
A penguin can stay submerged ~~under water~~ for seven minutes.

submit an application, file an application

Rambling. Use the verb *apply*.
Did you ~~submit an application~~ apply for the job?
To be safe, you need to ~~file an application~~ apply now.

subsequently

Large word. The words *after*, *later*, or *then* are simpler word choices.

substantial

Inflated word. *Great* or *large* carry the same meaning.

substantiate

A flowery verb for *confirm*, *prove*, or *verify*.

subtle nuance

Repetition. Every *nuance* is *subtle*.
The sound was so clear every ~~subtle~~ nuance was heard.

successful victory

Redundant. A *victory* must be *successful*.
He recalled one ~~successful~~ victory back in the late 1980s.

successfully accomplish, successfully achieve, successfully pass

The adverb *successfully* is not always needed.
We ~~successfully~~ accomplished all last month's objectives.
His group helps people ~~successfully~~ achieve financial fitness.
Many will need help to ~~successfully~~ pass the written exam.

succinct overview, succinct summary, succinct synopsis

Overstated. All these modified words imply something already being *succinct*.
Today they're giving a(n) ~~succinct~~ overview to the company.
We need to give a ~~succinct~~ summary to the customers.
The report is intended as a ~~succinct~~ synopsis of the novel.

such being the case, that being the case

Dense. Use the word *so*.
And ~~such being the case~~ so, it's crucial to vote in the primary.
~~That being the case,~~ so I am apt to vote for someone else.

sudden collapse, sudden crisis, sudden explosion, sudden impulse, sudden urge, sudden whim

The word *sudden* is implied in each phrase and not needed.
The strong vibration caused a ~~sudden~~ collapse of the building.
The dollar's steep downturn caused a ~~sudden~~ crisis in Asia.
The climate caused a ~~sudden~~ pollen explosion into the air.
By no means was it a planned event, only ~~sudden~~ impulse.
To save fuel, she had a(n) ~~sudden~~ urge to buy a hybrid car.
On a ~~sudden~~ whim, they went to California for the holidays.

suffer with

See entry for **comfortable with**, **consult with**, **meet with**.

sufficient amount, sufficient enough, sufficient number of

Wordy. The words *enough* or *sufficient* can replace these phrases.
Our computer has a sufficient ~~amount of~~ hard drive space.
He has sufficient ~~enough~~ funds to open an IRA this year.
The hospital has ~~a sufficient number of~~ enough trained staff.

sum total

Repetition. Use *sum* or *total* but not both.
The ~~sum~~ total of her medical costs exceeds the allowance.

(the) summer season

Redundant. It's implied *summer* is a *season*.
She hopes to find a full-time job for ~~the~~ summer ~~season~~.

sunny outside

Excess. The word *sunny* is plenty.
It seldom gets too sunny ~~outside~~ in this part of the state.

superfluous

Complex word. *Extra, surplus*, or *unessential* are simpler.

superimposed over each other

Word overkill. Use the word *superimposed* by itself.
Images are superimposed ~~over each other~~ to show disparity.

supersede
Bulky. Try the word *replace*.

supplement (as a verb)
Elegant word. Try the word *add*.

support and help
Double nouns. Either word will do.
Your support ~~and help~~ for charity goes unmatched.

surge ahead
Extra word. *Surge* by itself will sometimes work.
After the earnings report, their stock is likely to surge ~~ahead~~.

surplus left over
Repetition. *Surplus* alone will do.
He inherited a surplus ~~left over~~ from the prior administration.

surprise pop quiz, surprise upset
Redundant. *Pop quizzes* and *upsets* are always *surprises*.
The professor gave us a ~~surprise~~ pop quiz yesterday.
The candidate's ~~surprise~~ upset had many talking last night.

surreptitious
Fancy word. *Covert, secret*, *sly*, or *sneaky* are simpler choices.

surrounded on all sides
Overstated. Use the verb *surrounded*.
The tough golf hole was surrounded ~~on all sides~~ by water.

surrounding circumstances, surrounding environment
Redundant modifiers. *Surrounding* is assumed.
He is studying the ~~surrounding~~ circumstances of her death.
The smog causes harm to the ~~surrounding~~ environment.

surviving widow
Redundant. A *widow* is a *survivor*.
The proceeds of the insurance went to his ~~surviving~~ widow.

sweet fragrance

Redundant. A *fragrance* must be *sweet*.
Gardenias provide a natural, ~~sweet~~ fragrance for perfumes.

swirling around

Redundant. *Swirling* typically implies going *around*.
Layoff rumors continue to be swirling ~~around~~ the workplace.

switchblade knife

Redundant. A *switchblade* is a *knife*.
Some states have laws for carrying a switchblade ~~knife~~.

systematic

Complex word. The word *orderly* is simpler.

T

"As to the adjective, when in doubt, strike it out."—Mark Twain

tactful diplomacy

Redundant. *Diplomacy* should always be *tactful*.
The official's ~~tactful~~ diplomacy convinced us we were wrong.

take action, take appropriate measures

Verbose. Trim these phrases to simply the verb *act*.
~~Take action~~ act now on your career before it's too late.
We will ~~take appropriate measures~~ act so the process is fair.

take cognizance of, take notice of

Chatty. The verbs *heed*, *note*, or *notice* carry the same meaning.
The high court may ~~take cognizance of~~ note this offense.
Producers are beginning to ~~take~~ notice ~~of~~ the new talent.

take into consideration

Fatty phrases. The words *consider* or *therefore* are leaner.
Please ~~take into consideration~~ consider our proposal.

take it offline

Industry jargon. Try using the phrase *discuss that later*.
Good comment, but we will ~~take it offline~~ discuss that later.

take this opportunity to

Verbal surplus. This phrase can usually be omitted.
I want to ~~take this opportunity to~~ thank anyone who helped.

talking out loud, laughing out loud

Chatty. The phrase *out loud* can be removed.
Most libraries prohibit talking ~~out loud~~ in the corridors.
The students were caught laughing ~~out loud~~ in class.

(the) temperature of

Excess. At times, this phrase can be discarded.
~~The temperature of~~ the classroom is almost 68 degrees.

temporary loan, temporary recess, temporary reprieve, temporary stopgap

Unneeded modifiers. *Temporary* is already implied.
The ~~temporary~~ loan request should be sent immediately.
He has the power to make a ~~temporary~~ recess appointment.
We received a ~~temporary~~ reprieve on the past due balance.
We relied on ~~temporary~~ stopgap staffing until hiring resumed.

tenacious

Determined, firm, persistent, or *resolute* are simpler word choices.

tend to

Extra words. A phrase often removed.
Allocation of public funds ~~tend to~~ favor the ruling parties.

tendered their resignations

Rambling. Use the phrase *they resigned*.
Amid controversy, they ~~tendered their resignations~~ resigned.

tentatively suggested

Overdone. The adverb *tentatively* is not needed.
We ~~tentatively~~ suggested our meeting be delayed.

terminate

Prefer the simpler verbs *cancel, cease, end*, or *stop*.

terrible disaster, terrible tragedy

Redundant. *Disasters* and *tragedies* are always *terrible*.
A ~~terrible~~ flood disaster almost occurred in that town.
The town was lucky to avoid a ~~terrible~~ tragedy.

thank you for your cooperation in this matter, thank you in advance

Trite business letter phrases. Use the phrase *thank you* instead.

We sincerely thank you ~~for your cooperation in this matter~~.

Thank you ~~in advance~~ for bringing the error to our attention.

thanks and gratitude

Double nouns. Either word will do.

Please give our sincere thanks ~~and gratitude~~ to the team.

that

This relative pronoun can often be cut.

Ed will drop the class, provided ~~that~~ he gets permission.

They knew ~~that~~ they could get excellent results.

Where are the files ~~that~~ you want put into storage?

Note: Sometimes you cannot delete the word *that* because it changes the intended meaning.

He felt ~~that~~ his foot. . . .

that being the case

See entry for **such being the case**.

that exists

Excess. This phrase can be omitted.

The inequity ~~that exists~~ between the groups is not right.

that have been

Wordy. Often this phrase can be deleted.

Ideas ~~that have been~~ studied for years are being enacted.

that is, that was, that were

Verbose. Often, relative pronouns and their verbs can be cut.

Use the process ~~that is~~ essential for your business plan.

The tool ~~that was~~ developed last year received a patent.

The monies ~~that were~~ collected went toward local charities.

therapeutic treatment

Verbal surplus. Usually this is an unneeded modifier.
Honey is used as a ~~therapeutic~~ treatment for many ailments.

there are, there is, there was, there were

Extra words. These phrases, coupled with *which*, *who*, or *that* can often be cut.
~~There are~~ some people ~~who~~ never attend this ceremony.
~~There is~~ a lovely river ~~that~~ runs through the city.
~~There was~~ a loud noise ~~which~~ shook the houses.
~~There were~~ four issues ~~that~~ still need addressing.

Sometimes the phrase by itself is unnecessary.

If you suspect ~~there is~~ a problem, try to fix it.
Before ~~there was~~ the Internet, the library was more popular.

there can be little doubt that

Long-winded. The word *probably* can replace this phrase.
~~There can be little doubt that~~ probably they are at fault.

these are areas that

Verbose. The phrase *these areas* carries the same meaning.
These ~~are~~ areas ~~that~~ in the house need a major overhaul.

they are in fact

Overstated. At times, the phrase *in fact* can be cut.
They are ~~in fact~~ the more compassionate political party.

they themselves

Repetition. Omit the word *themselves*.
She realizes they ~~themselves~~ also believe in miracles.

thin veneer

Redundant. Any *veneer* is *thin*.
Natural ~~thin~~ veneer stone is durable and quicker to install.

think outside the box

Industry jargon. Try phrases like *be creative* or *be original*.
To remain competitive, try to ~~think outside the box~~ be creative.

thinking to myself

Excess. The phrase *to myself* is not needed.
I was thinking ~~to myself~~ this will be a night to remember.

this is a subject that, this is an area that

Wordy. The phrases *this subject* and *this area* are simpler.
This ~~is a~~ subject ~~that~~ gets debated every year.
This ~~is an~~ area ~~that~~ needs serious improvement.

this is to acknowledge and thank you

Long-winded. The phrase *thank you* is less wordy.
~~This is to acknowledge and~~ thank you for your inquiry.

this is to say that, this translates to

Roundabout. The phrase *this means* is more direct.
This ~~is to say that~~ means all checks are accepted here.
With higher octane, this ~~translates to~~ means better mileage.

this particular instance

Tedious. The word *particular* is often not needed.
In this ~~particular~~ instance, we see a clear marketing failure.

this time around

Chatty. The word *around* can often be cut.
This time ~~around~~ I'll know what questions to ask them.

thought and consideration, thoughts and ideas

Redundant nouns. Choose only one word from each phrase.
After much ~~thought and~~ consideration, we will attend.
Send us your thoughts ~~and ideas~~ on this new approach.

throughout the course of, throughout the duration of

Wordy. The word *throughout* by itself is plenty.
Macbeth's nature changes throughout ~~the course of~~ the play.
Cell phones are not on throughout ~~the duration of~~ a flight.

throw it against the wall and see what sticks
Tired cliché meaning to present an idea and test its reaction.

time clock, time deadline, time period, time schedule
Redundant modifiers. The word *time* is already implied.
He still uses the ~~time~~ clock to punch in each day.
What is the ~~time~~ deadline for submitting our responses?
We're free to choose any ~~time~~ period in history for our essay.
Here is the projected ~~time~~ schedule for delivering our reports.

time interval
Overstated. The noun *interval* can be omitted.
The time ~~interval~~ from submission to printing is short.

time of day
Word padding. The phrase *of day* is not necessary.
Experts disagree on the ideal time ~~of day~~ to exercise.

tiny
Tiny is an understood modifier in certain phrases.
The blood sample contained a ~~tiny~~ trace of radioactivity.

Other possibilities to consider include:

tiny bit	tiny infant
tiny detail	tiny iota
tiny duckling	tiny morsel
tiny dwarf	tiny particle
tiny fraction	tiny piece
tiny fragment	tiny sapling
tiny hamlet	tiny shred
tiny hint	tiny smidgen
tiny in stature	tiny speck

to
This preposition can be redundant at the end of a sentence.
Where are you going ~~to~~?
The children are free to name the pet any name they want ~~to~~.

to a large degree, to a large extent

Long-winded. Try the word *mainly*.
~~To a large degree,~~ mainly his research findings are misread.
We did it ~~to a large extent,~~ mainly to help the storm victims.

to be, to do

Verbal surplus. Often these phrases can be removed.
At first glance, this assignment appears ~~to be~~ difficult.
Keeping your composure during a debate can be tough ~~to do~~.

to be perfectly honest

Muddle. This phrase seldom adds anything. Delete it.
~~To be perfectly honest~~ I cannot answer your question.

to have

Excess. Often this phrase can be cut.
We need ~~to have~~ new procedures to improve our quality.

to summarize the above

Verbose. Say *in summary*.
~~To summarize the above~~ in summary, the cost is too high.

to the extent that

Word padding. Use the words *if* or *when*.
~~To the extent that~~ if we do not succeed, I'll be to blame.

to the fullest possible extent

Lengthy. Use *fully* or delete the entire phrase.
Your identity is protected ~~to the fullest possible extent~~ fully.

to whatever extent

Rambling. At times, the word *however* can replace this phrase.
Influence their decision ~~to whatever extent~~ however you can.

together

The word *together* can be dropped if used with verb phrases that imply something done *together*.

They collaborated ~~together~~ with other students on the project.
They developed aptitude tests that do correlate ~~together~~.
The relatives would gather ~~together~~ each year for a reunion.
We will all meet ~~together~~ downtown after the movie.

Other possibilities to consider include:

add together	couple together
aggregate together	fasten together
all meet together	flock together
associate together	fuse together
attach together	group together
blend together	huddle together
bond together	integrate together
bundle together	intertwined together
cluster together	join together
cobble together	liaise together
cohabit together	link together
collect together	merge together
combine together	mesh together
compile together	mingle together
concatenated together	mix together
confer together	pack together
congregate together	share together
connect together	splice together
consolidate together	stack together
convene together	string together
converge together	unite together
cooperate together	weave together
corroborate together	weld together

together at the same time

Overstated. The phrase *at the same time* can be cut.
To do a command, press the keys together ~~at the same time~~.

top capacity

Redundant. *Capacity* means at the *top*.
Surprisingly our old computer still runs at ~~top~~ capacity.

total

Excess introductory word.
The buffalo was once feared for ~~total~~ extinction.

Other examples to consider include:

total abstinence	total destruction
total annihilation	total number
total chaos	total reversal

(a) total of

This phrase can sometimes be omitted.
Our company received ~~a total of~~ 10 new patent applications.

totally

A redundant qualifier in a phrase such as:
She is eligible for six months of ~~totally~~ free Internet service.

Other phrases to consider include:

totally annihilated	totally empty
totally blind	totally exhausted
totally committed	totally full
totally deaf	totally obvious
totally demolished	totally overwhelmed
totally destroyed	totally unanimous
totally devoted	totally unnecessary

totally and completely

Redundant adverbs. Pick just one.
They are ~~totally and~~ completely right on the issues.

tough challenge

Redundant. All *challenges* are *tough*.
To continue its streak, the team faces a ~~tough~~ challenge.

toward the direction of, in the direction of

Chatty. Say *toward*.
The errant shot went toward ~~the direction of~~ the spectators.
The errant shot headed ~~in the direction of~~ toward the crowd.

toxic mercury, toxic poison

Redundant. *Mercury* and *poisons* are *toxic* things.
The CFL bulbs contain 6 to 8 milligrams of ~~toxic~~ mercury.
The bacteria can often produce a powerful ~~toxic~~ poison.

toys and playthings

Redundant nouns. One of these words will do.
Many toys ~~and playthings~~ offer kids a chance to learn.

track record

Unneeded modifier. Go with just the word *record*.
We checked their ~~track~~ record before enlisting their help.

trail behind

*See entry for **follow behind, lag behind, leave behind.***

transcribe

Bulky word. The verb *copy* is simpler.

travel around

Word overkill. The verb *travel* alone is usually plenty.
Our goal has always been to travel ~~around~~ the entire U.S.

traversed across

Tedious. The word *across* is an unneeded preposition.
The climbers traversed ~~across~~ the east face of the mountain.

trite cliché

Redundant. All *clichés* are *trite*.
"Agree to disagree" is sometimes seen as a ~~trite~~ cliché.

true and accurate, true and correct

Repetition. Choose one or the other but not both.
We certify the above statements are true ~~and accurate~~.
The statement given in court is ~~true and~~ correct.

true fact

Redundant. *Facts* have to be *true.*
A thorough investigation will yield the ~~true~~ facts of the case.

truly sincere

Needless modifier. *Sincere* should not be qualified.
Her talk was not only motivational but ~~truly~~ sincere.

trust implicitly

Needless adverb. Omit *implicitly.*
It's important to have friends whom you can trust ~~implicitly~~.

truth and veracity

Overstated. Either word will do.
Among her friends, she's known for her truth ~~and veracity~~.

truthfully

Overused modifier that adds little and can be deleted.
We can ~~truthfully~~ say it was the best decision we made.

tuition cost, tuition fees

Redundant. *Tuition* implies *costs* and *fees.*
The tuition ~~costs~~ at many four-year colleges is rising.
One benefit is having the company pay my tuition ~~fees~~.

twelve (12) midnight, twelve (12) noon

Redundancies. The words *midnight* and *noon* will do.
We left the gathering by ~~12~~ noon.

two different

Extra word. The adjective *different* is not needed.
The scientist found two ~~different~~ types of lava in the crater.
They had two ~~different~~ views on the new policy.

two equal halves

Lengthy. The word *equal* is unnecessary.
The deck of cards was split into two ~~equal~~ halves.

two-person tandem

Unneeded modifier. *Tandem* implies *two*.
We use ~~two-person~~ tandem sea kayaks at the lake.

type of

Excess. Often this phrase can be cut.
The board is careful on the ~~type of~~ policies they propose.

U

"I want to write books that unlock the traffic jam in everybody's head."—John Updike

ugly blemish

Redundant. *Blemishes* are assumed to be *ugly*.
By re-dyeing the carpet, we did remove the ~~ugly~~ blemish.

ultimate

Ultimate is often a needless modifying word.
He maintains there is an ~~ultimate~~ end to human existence.

Other possibilities to consider include:

ultimate climax	ultimate goal
ultimate completion	ultimate limit
ultimate conclusion	ultimate outcome
ultimate culmination	ultimate settlement
ultimate farewell	ultimate upshot

unanimous

This word can stand on its own and *not be qualified* in phrases such as:

completely unanimous	totally unanimous
fully unanimous	utterly unanimous
thoroughly unanimous	wholly unanimous

unaware of the fact that

Rambling. To be more concise, use the word *unaware*.
We were unaware ~~of the fact that~~ you were leaving us.

uncertainty

Big word for the simpler word *doubt*.

uncommonly strange

Redundant. Something *uncommon* is *strange*.
How he eluded the law for so long is ~~uncommonly~~ strange.

unconfirmed rumor, unfounded rumor, unsubstantiated rumor, baseless rumor

Redundant. *Rumors* are always *unconfirmed*, *unfounded*, *unsubstantiated*, and *baseless*.
~~Unconfirmed~~ rumors report PCs will see price cuts this year.
~~Unfounded~~ rumors about the company sale were rampant.
The ~~unsubstantiated~~ rumor started right after he left politics.
The report was false and viewed as a ~~baseless~~ rumor.

undeniable truth

Redundant. The *truth* is always *undeniable*.
Job growth is the ~~undeniable~~ truth about her first term.

under circumstances in which

Long-winded. Pare this phrase to simply *if* or *when*.
~~Under circumstances in which~~ when costs climb, I cut back.

under separate cover

Trite business phrase. Use the word *separately*.
The bidding rules appear ~~under separate cover~~ separately.

under the provisions of

Chatty. Use the words *of* or *under*.
We can waive tuition under ~~the provisions of~~ the new order.

underage minor

Redundant. A *minor* is a person *underage*.
Rules prohibit ~~underage~~ minors from entering the casino.

undergraduate student

Repetition. *Undergraduate* by itself is fine.
He is an undergraduate ~~student~~ at State College, Potsdam.

underground subway, underground tunnel

Redundant. *Subways* and *tunnels* are *underground*.
Take the ~~underground~~ subway to Grand Central Station.
The college has ~~underground~~ tunnels under the campus.

undertake a study of

Tedious. The verb *study* will do.
The students will ~~undertake a~~ study ~~of~~ different cultures.

undertake an analysis of

Long-winded. Try the verb *analyze*.
He will ~~undertake an analysis of~~ analyze the new policy.

undisclosed secret location

Word overkill. All *secret locations* are *undisclosed*.
The ~~undisclosed~~ secret location is used for high officials.

unduly forced

Verbal surplus. The word *forced* by itself is plenty.
The lyrics are catchy without any ~~unduly~~ forced rhymes.

unequivocal

Inflated word. Try the word *clear*.

unexpected emergency, unexpected surprise, unexpected twist

Redundant. These situations are always *unexpected*.
Short-term loans are available for ~~unexpected~~ emergencies.
Low interest rates were an ~~unexpected~~ surprise to investors.
His stories often have a sudden ~~unexpected~~ twist at the end.

uniformly consistent, uniformly homogeneous

Excess. The word *uniformly* is unnecessary.
He now hits the golf ball more ~~uniformly~~ consistent than ever.
From here, the earth's surface looks ~~uniformly~~ homogeneous.

unintentional accident, unintentional mistake, unintentional oversight

Redundant. All three things are always *unintentional*.
The ~~unintentional~~ accident almost led to serious injury.
His ~~unintentional~~ mistake on the math test cost him greatly.
Not notifying them at once was an ~~unintentional~~ oversight.

uninvited intruder

Redundant. *Intruders* are always *uninvited*.
The Police confronted the ~~uninvited~~ intruder immediately.

unique

This word means *one of a kind*, so it's illogical to qualify it.
Her approach to solving the math problem was ~~fairly~~ unique.

Other examples to consider include:

completely unique	so unique
especially unique	somewhat unique
extremely unique	totally unique
highly unique	truly unique
more unique	utterly unique
most unique	very unique
quite unique	

unique and one of a kind, unique in its own way

Overstated. The word *unique* by itself is fine.
The house is unique ~~and one of a kind~~ for this urban area.
Her golf swing is strong, smooth, and unique ~~in its own way~~.

uniquely different

Redundant. The word *different* implies *unique*.
Each hotel suite is ~~uniquely~~ different in layout and size.

united as one

Wordy. At times, the phrase *as one* is not needed.
We set aside our political differences to be united ~~as one~~.

universal panacea

Redundant. *Panacea* implies being *universal*.
He feels melatonin is a candidate for a ~~universal~~ panacea.

unknown stranger

Redundant. *Strangers* are always *unknown*.
An ~~unknown~~ stranger greeted us at the town meeting.

unless and until

Repetition. Choose either word but not both.
The ban is valid unless ~~and until~~ outdated by a new order.

unloosen, unpeel, unthaw

Surplus. The prefix *un* is not needed.
Simply ~~un~~loosen the wheel and apply some lubricant.
~~Un~~peeling a golf ball cover can be tricky and messy.
You'll have to give the frozen meat time to ~~un~~thaw.

unneeded luxury, unneeded verbiage

Overstated. Drop the word *unneeded*.
For some, the Blackberry is a~~n~~ ~~unneeded~~ luxury.
Trim the ~~unneeded~~ verbiage from your business writing.

unoccupied

Large word. Try the simpler word *empty*.

unpleasant odor, foul odor

Redundant. *Odors* are *unpleasant* and *foul*.
An ~~unpleasant~~ odor continues to come from the landfill.
If you smell a(n) ~~foul~~ odor, immediately open a window.

unproved allegation, unsubstantiated allegation

Redundant. *Allegations* are always *unproved* or *unsubstantiated*.
The ~~unproved~~ allegation of abuse was one of the issues.
A record check refuted the ~~unsubstantiated~~ allegation.

unrealized potential

Redundant. *Potential* is always *unrealized*.
The teacher tapped the ~~unrealized~~ potential of her students.

unsafe hazard

Redundant. *Hazards* are understood to be *unsafe*.
She recognized the ~~unsafe~~ hazards but didn't alert anyone.

unsolved mystery, unsolved problem

Redundant. *Mysteries* and *problems* are always unsolved.
The USS Scorpion's sinking remains an ~~unsolved~~ mystery.
He's interested in ~~unsolved~~ problems in set theory and logic.

until such time as

Long-winded. Use the word *until* by itself.
Schools are closed until ~~such time as~~ the weather improves.

untimely death

Redundant. All *deaths* are *untimely*.
Any ~~untimely~~ death is usually a bad memory for someone.

unusual in nature

Verbose. The word *unusual* is plenty.
Losses in their financial statements are unusual ~~in nature~~.

unwanted spam

Redundant. *Spam* is assumed to be *unwanted*.
Protect your computer from ~~unwanted~~ spam and viruses.

up

Up is usually a needless ending preposition in a verb phrase.
If it works as designed, the phone will charge ~~up~~ in minutes.
The teacher came to check ~~up~~ on our weekly progress.
Their county is a good place for children to grow ~~up~~.
They're trying to save ~~up~~ for their first house.
The two retailers will team ~~up~~ to market the new product.

Other examples to consider include:

add up	draw up	lift up	shore up
advance up	dream up	link up	shrivel up
ascend up	dress up	load up	sit up
back up	drink up	look up	speed up
bandage up	drive up	loosen up	spruce up
botch up	eat up	match up	staff up
bought up	elevate up	measure up	stand up
bubble up	end up	mess up	start up
buckle up	face up to	mount up	stir up
build up	fill up	offer up	straighten up
burn up	finish up	open up	study up
buy up	fired up	order up	tense up
call them up	firm up	packaged up	tidy up
call up	fix up	paired up	tighten up
chew up	fold up	partner up	took up
choose up	force up	pay up	total up
chop up	free it up	pile up	tune up
clean up	freed up	polish up	type up
close up	freeze up	push up	use up
cloud it up	gather up	raise up	vacuum up
clutter up	gear up	ramp up	wait up
coming up	gum up	ratchet up	wake up
conjure up	hatched up	rest up	write up
connect up	head up	rewind up	
cook up	heat up	rile up	
count up	hitch up	rise up	
cover up	hoist up	saddle up	
creep up	hurry up	send it up	
cut up	increase up	serve up	
divide up	join up	settle up	

up and running

Redundant. If it's *up*, it is usually *running* and vice versa.
The system will be ~~up and~~ running in a minute.

up in the attic, up in the sky, up on the roof

Overstated. The preposition *up* is not needed; it's implied.
Anne Frank and her family lived ~~up~~ in the attic for three years.
"Look, ~~up~~ in the sky, it's a bird, it's a plane; no, it's Superman"!
Back in the 1970s, we installed solar panels ~~up~~ on the roof.

up to this time, up until that time

Chatty. Use the phrase *until then*.
~~Up to this time~~, until then, we lacked any idea of what to do.
~~Up~~ until ~~that time~~ then, good ideas were lacking from us.

upon further consideration

Long-winded. Use the word *now*.
But ~~upon further consideration~~ now, it may be a wise option.

upon receipt of

Clutter. A tired, business phrase we can cut.
~~Upon receipt of~~ when we get the check, we will notify you.

upward

Overstated. Shorten the word to *up*.
As the antenna goes up~~ward~~, the signal definitely improves.

use and implementation

Overdone. Go with just the word *use*.
I'm studying the use ~~and implementation~~ of a weight loss pill.

use of

Excess. Often this phrase can be removed.
Her ~~use of~~ excellent examples explain it much more clearly.

used in preference to

Rambling. The phrase *preferable to* is tighter.
Natural materials are ~~used in preference~~ preferable to plastic.

useless and unnecessary

Redundant adjectives. Choose one or the other but not both.
We received some useless ~~and unnecessary~~ stock advice.

uses and applications

Redundant nouns. Choose one or the other but not both.
Ascorbic acid has many industrial ~~applications and~~ uses.

usual custom, usual habit

Overstated. The word *usual* is not needed.
Eggnog during the holiday season is their ~~usual~~ custom.
The author's ~~usual~~ habit is to use many small words.

utmost perfection

Verbal surplus. The noun *perfection* cannot be qualified.
The auto shop restored the classic car to ~~utmost~~ perfection.

utter and complete

See entry for **complete and full, complete and utter**.

utterly rejected

Extra word. *Utterly* is an unneeded qualifier.
Competent scientists ~~utterly~~ rejected their unusual theory.

utilize

Complex word. The word *use* is much simpler.

V

"Parenthetical remarks (however relevant) are unnecessary."—
Frank L. Visco

vacillating back and forth
Redundant. It's assumed this motion is *back and forth*.
After vacillating ~~back and forth~~, she applied for the job.

validate
Inflated word. The word *prove* is simpler.

valuable asset
Redundant. All *assets* are *valuable*.
Innovation will always be a(n) ~~valuable~~ asset here.

value added
Overworked business phrase. Delete the word *added*.
What is the value ~~added~~ of hiring more employees now?

(the) value of
Empty phrase. At times, this whole phrase can be cut.
Adjust ~~the value of~~ the recording level before you start.

various and sundry
Repetition. Choose one or the other but not both.
I bought many various ~~and sundry~~ items over the holidays.

various differences, various kinds, various varieties
Word overkill. The word *various* is not needed.
~~Various~~ differences exist between Version 1 and Version 2.
Many ~~various~~ kinds of vegetables are available at the market.
~~Various~~ varieties of vegetables are available to consumers.

(the) vast majority of the

Long-winded. Say *most*.
~~The vast majority of the~~ *most people agree with the rule.*

venerable

Stuffy word. *Admired, honored*, or *revered* are simpler choices.

venture a guess, venture a suggestion

Roundabout. The verbs *guess* and *suggest* are more direct.
Let me ~~venture a~~ *guess how many people will attend tonight.*
I ~~venture a suggestion~~ *suggest we delay the grand opening.*

veracious

Heavy word. Try using *true* instead.

verbally spoken

Redundant. If it's *spoken*, it's *verbal*.
Not all languages are ~~verbally~~ *spoken.*

vertical dive, vertical drop

Redundant. All *dives* and *drops* are *vertical*.
The aircraft managed to pull out of its sudden ~~vertical~~ *dive.*
The slope has a ~~vertical~~ *drop of 95 feet and a run of 600 feet.*

very

A much overused intensifier that can be deleted and often
replaced with a synonym.
My ~~very~~ *favorite class this semester is English Literature.*
We made our ~~very last~~ *final attempt to contact them.*

Other possibilities to consider include:

very abnormal – unusual
very affordable – reasonable
very afraid – scared
very amused – entertained
very bad – awful
very beautiful – gorgeous

very best – optimum
very big – huge, large
very bothersome – annoying
very brave – heroic
very brief – short
very bright – intelligent, smart
very brittle – delicate
very careful – deliberate
very cheap – stingy
very cold – frigid
very complicated – complex
very costly – expensive
very critical – important
very definitely - yes
very detailed – explicit
very different – unusual
very difficult – tough
very easy – simple
very encouraged - optimistic
very excited – elated
very familiar – common, well-known
very few – few
very flattering - complimentary
very frequently – often
very funny – amusing, hilarious
very generous – benevolent
very good – exceptional
very grateful – grateful, thankful
very happy – elated
very honest – trustworthy
very hungry – starving, famished
very important – critical or vital
very large – huge
very late – tardy
very latest – current, recent
very likely – probable
very many – many
very nice – pleasant
very noisy – loud

very often – often
very old – ancient
very poor – destitute
very popular – famous, well-known
very positive – optimistic
very powerful – strong
very pretty – gorgeous, attractive
very quick – fast, speedy
very rapidly – fast
very rich – wealthy
very roomy – spacious
very selective – fussy
very short – brief, succinct
very similar – like
very skinny – thin
very slowly – crawled
very small – tiny
very smart – intelligent
very soon – imminent
very sophisticated – complex
very sorry – apologetic
very substantial – large
very sweet – sugary
very tired – exhausted
very typical – common
very uncommon – rare
very unhappy – miserable
very unnecessary - trivial
very unusual – rare
very warm – hot, humid, or muggy
very worried – concerned
very wrong – incorrect

viable

Overworked word as in *viable alternative* or *viable solution*.
Use *possible*, *practicable*, or *workable* instead.

views and opinions

Redundant nouns. Pick one.
He promises to consider the ~~views and~~ opinions of voters.

violent battle, fierce battle

Redundant. Battles are *violent* or *fierce*.
Congress waged a ~~fierce~~ battle over the latest spending bill.

violent explosion

Redundant. Any *explosion* is *violent*.
~~A violent~~ an explosion destroyed the building instantly.

virtually

Word overkill. This word seldom adds anything.
Our sales estimates for the year are ~~virtually~~ unchanged.

visible to the eye

Overstated. The phrase *to the eye* is excess.
Uranus is usually visible ~~to the eye~~ on a clear night.

visual sight

Redundant. The word *sight* implies something *visual*.
As I've aged, my ~~visual~~ sight has deteriorated.

visualize

Flowery word. Use the simpler verbs *picture* or *see*.

vitally important, vitally necessary

Redundant. If they're *important* and *necessary*, they're *vital*.
The experience is ~~vitally~~ important to his professional career.
Proper safeguarding for all our schools is ~~vitally~~ necessary.

vocal and vociferous

Repetition. Choose one or the other but not both.
The customers are also their most vocal ~~and vociferous~~ critics.

voiced disapproval of

Overstated. The phrase *disapproved of* is simpler.
They ~~voiced disapproval of~~ disapproved of the downsizing.

volley back and forth

Redundant. A *volley* implies going *back and forth*.
Stand near the net and volley ~~back and forth~~ to each other.

voluminous

Large word. Try the simpler words *big*, *hefty*, *huge*, or *large.*

voting ballot

Redundant. *Voting* involves *ballots*.
She succeeded in getting her name on the ~~voting~~ ballot.

"Use the smallest word that does the job."—E.B. White

waffle back and forth
Overstated. Omit the ending phrase.
Instead of waffling ~~back and forth~~ on the issues, stand firm.

wait around
Surplus ending preposition. Delete the word *around*.
Do not wait ~~around~~ for the fax. It could be hours.

wall mural
Redundant. *Murals* must be on *walls*.
Painting a ~~wall~~ mural is an exciting way to decorate a room.

warn ahead, warn in advance
Redundant. *Warnings* are always given *ahead* or *in advance*.
Be sure to warn them ~~ahead~~ of any expected problems.
They didn't warn us ~~in advance~~ of the looming weather.

was aware of
See entry for **be aware of, is aware of**.

was witness to
Long-winded. Try the simpler word *saw*.
He ~~was witness to~~ saw the entire accident from his office.

watching and observing
Redundant verbs. One of these words will do.
Animals learn from watching ~~and observing~~ other animals.

water hydrant, fire hydrant
Redundant. *Hydrants* can pertain to *water* or *fire*.
Illegally using a ~~water~~ hydrant may jeopardize fire fighting.

we acknowledge receipt of

Stale business phrase. Prefer the simpler: *Thank you for…*

we are pleased to advise that

Stale business phrase we can often omit.
~~We are pleased to advise that~~ you have been accepted.

we are returning herewith

Rambling. Trim this phrase to *enclosed is*.
~~We are returning herewith~~ enclosed is the completed form.

we are submitting

Bulky phrase for *here is* or *here are*.
Unfortunately, ~~we are submitting~~ here are our resignations.

we can assure you

Verbose. The word *certainly* could replace this phrase.
~~We can assure you~~ certainly the experience was worth it.

we now think it likely that

Long-winded. Use the word *probably*.
~~We now think it likely that~~ probably she'll return next year.

we ourselves

Repetition. The word *ourselves* is unnecessary.
With technology, we ~~ourselves~~ must remain current.

we regret to advise

Tired business phrase. The word *unfortunately* can replace this.
~~We regret to advise~~ unfortunately all tickets are sold.

we trust this is satisfactory

Stale business phrase. Prefer using *we hope you are happy*.

we wish to apologize

Roundabout. *We apologize* is more direct.
We ~~wish to~~ apologize for any inconvenience.

we wish to take this opportunity to thank you

Roundabout. The phrase *thank you* is more direct.

we would appreciate it if you could

Excessive. The word *please* carries the same meaning.
~~We would appreciate it if you could~~ please give us feedback.

wealthy millionaire, wealthy philanthropist

Redundant. *Millionaires* and *philanthropists* are *wealthy*.
When he won the lottery, he became a ~~wealthy~~ millionaire.
The ~~wealthy~~ philanthropist donated millions to charities.

weather conditions

Word overkill. The word *conditions* can be deleted.
The bad weather ~~conditions~~ postponed last week's game.

weave in and out

Wordy. The word *weave* by itself will work.
The test car did weave ~~in and out~~ between all the pylons.

went on to say

Chatty. The words *added* or *continued* are briefer.
He ~~went on to say~~ added how grateful he was for the help.

what I mean to say is that

Word padding. This empty phrase is typically not needed.
~~What I mean to say is that~~ people always make mistakes.

what is the name of the

Rambling. Usually *which* or *who* can replace this phrase.
What is the name of the hotel? vs. **Which** hotel?
What is the name of the person you know? vs. **Who** do you know?

when all is said and done

Empty phrasing. Try using *all in all*.
~~When all is said and done~~, all in all, we like living here.

when and if

Verbal overload. Typically one of these words will do.
We will update the file when ~~and if~~ we get their feedback.

whether or not

Excess. The word *whether* by itself is sometimes plenty.
Whether ~~or not~~ she is our first president is not the issue.

which is, which was

Tedious. Often, relative pronouns and their verbs can be deleted.
The book, ~~which is~~ new this year, is already a hit in stores.
A movie, ~~which was~~ popular last year, is back in theaters.

while at the same time, while simultaneously

Word overkill. Use the word *while*.
I found time to study while ~~at the same time~~ working two jobs.
He improved service while ~~simultaneously~~ reducing costs.

whispered softly

Redundant. How else would one whisper?
"Never give up," she whispered ~~softly~~ into his ear.

who are, who is, whom are, whom is

Tedious. Often, relative pronouns and their verbs can be cut.
People ~~who are~~ at high risk~~,~~ shouldn't take this drug.
John, ~~who is~~ a SUNY graduate, applied for the position.
The people ~~whom are~~ going to the event, ….
The person ~~whom~~ you know ~~is~~, ….

(a) whole lot

Overstated. *Whole* is an extra word that adds little.
Her writing style made the book a ~~whole~~ lot more compelling.

why

Excess. Sometimes this word can be cut.
The reason ~~why~~ the TV show is failing is lack of interest.

(a) wide range of, a wide variety of

Chatty. The words *many* and *different* say the same thing.
Smoking can cause ~~a wide range of~~ many health problems.
The new tool supports ~~a wide variety of~~ different applications.

widow of the late

Verbal surplus. The phrase *the late* can be dropped.
The widow of ~~the late~~ John Smith still lives in California.

wild pandemonium, wild savage

Redundant. *Pandemonium* and *savage* are *wild*.
The star's arrival was greeted with ~~wild~~ pandemonium.
The story centers on a ~~wild~~ savage beast from the jungle.

wilderness area

Overstated. The word *wilderness* is usually enough.
The large wilderness ~~area~~ runs through three counties.

will be of assistance

Verbose. The phrase *will help* is more concise.
Counselors will ~~be of assistance~~ help during the week.

will not be allowed to

Long-winded. The word *cannot* means the same.
Cameras ~~will not be allowed to~~ cannot be in the courtroom.

willing volunteer

Redundant. All *volunteers* are *willingly*.
We need a ~~willing~~ volunteer to join a scientific expedition.

willingly agreed

Redundant. If you *agree* to something, it's done *willingly*.
She has ~~willingly~~ agreed to accept blame for the errors.

(the) winter season

Overstated. It's implied *winter* is a *season*.
We enjoy skiing and hockey in ~~the~~ winter ~~season~~.

wish to state our

Empty expression often omitted.
We ~~wish to state our~~ have concern for the elderly.

with

Extra word. If used as a pointless ending preposition, omit.
We'll get together when the meeting is over ~~with~~.

with a view to, with a view toward

Long-winded. Phrases often replaced with the words *for* or *to*.
She took the assignment ~~with a view~~ to further her career.
I'm saving now ~~with a view toward~~ for fiscal security later.

with due consideration

Stale business phrase. Try to avoid.

with reference to, with regard to, with relation to, with respect to

Chatty. The word *about* can replace these phrases.
~~With reference to~~ about your question, doors open at 8 p.m.
He knows something ~~with regard to~~ about the missing cash.
The attorney knows details ~~with relation to~~ about this case.
They wrote to us ~~with respect to~~ about financing details.

with the aid of

Overstated. Replace this phrase with simply *with*.
With ~~the aid of~~ an interpreter, the leaders communicated.

with the knowledge that

Rambling. Use the word *knowing*.
I play ~~with the knowledge that~~ knowing I may be injured.

with the minimum of delay

Muddle. Replace this wordy expression with simply *quickly*.
Please respond to us ~~with the minimum of delay~~ quickly.

with the possible exception of
Overstated. The phrase *except for* carries the same meaning.
~~With the possible exception of~~ except for me, all attended.

with the result that
Long-winded. Try using *so* instead.
Can I resize the image ~~with the result that~~ so it will upload?

with this in mind
Excessive. The word *therefore* means the same.
~~With this in mind~~ therefore it would be wise to invest early.

within the ballpark of
Lengthy. Say *about*, *almost*, *around*, *nearly*, or *roughly*.
We live ~~within the ballpark of~~ almost 10 minutes away.

without any major effect
Tedious. The word *any* can be removed.
The merger was without ~~any~~ major effect to the workforce.

without further delay
Word padding. This phrase can often be omitted.
And now, ~~without further delay,~~ please meet our new CEO.

witnessed first-hand
Redundant. *Witnessing* something is *first-hand*.
We witnessed ~~first-hand~~ the many benefits of living there.

wordy and verbose
Redundant adjectives. Choose one or the other but not both.
The author's writing style tends to be wordy ~~and verbose~~.

would appreciate it if you, would you be so kind as to
Roundabout. The word *please* is simpler and more direct.
~~Would appreciate it if you could~~ please help me understand.
~~Would you be so kind as to~~ please direct me to an ATM.

would have to be

Chatty. The phrase *must be* is more concise.
Route 88 ~~would have to be~~ must be the quickest way to go.

written by author

Redundant. The *author* is the *writer*.
That publisher sells books written by ~~author~~ Maya Angelou.

written document, written script

Redundant. *Documents* and *scripts* must be written.
This paper discusses how to prepare all ~~written~~ documents.

Y

"It's never perfect when I write it the first time, or the second time, or the fifth time. But it always gets better as I go over it and over it."—Jane Yolen

yell and scream
Redundant verbs. Either word will do.
We have a rule never to yell ~~and scream~~ at the opponents.

yet however, yet nevertheless
Repetition. Delete one word or the other in each phrase.
I haven't finished the book; ~~yet~~ however, I've read most of it.
And yet ~~nevertheless~~, we are content with the outcome.

you are hereby advised that
Empty formal expression often removed.
~~You are hereby advised that~~ you have until Friday to apply.

you are in fact
Wordy. The phrase *in fact* is not needed.
You are ~~in fact~~ likely mistaken about the theory's origin.

you are requested to
Verbose. At times, the word *please* can replace this phrase.
~~You are requested~~ please ~~to~~ attend all three sessions.

you know
Useless and popular phrase that adds little.
~~You know,~~ she's interested in our ideas on emission control.
She's interested in our ideas on emission control~~, you know~~.

you yourself
Excess ending word.
Are you ~~yourself~~ covered by any health insurance at work?

young

Uncalled-for introductory word in phrases such as:

young adolescent	young juvenile
young baby	young kid
young colt	young kitten
young fawn	young lad
young foal	young lass
young infant	young puppy

your attention is drawn to

The simple phrases *please note* and *please see* are better.
~~Your attention is drawn to~~ *please see the new contract.*

youthful teenagers

Redundant. The word *youthful* is assumed.

Z

"Writing improves in direct ratio to the things we can keep out of it that shouldn't be there."—William Zinsser

zoom up

Zoom in and *zoom out* make sense, but *zoom up* is not logical.

About the Author

Dave Dowling is also the author of *The Wrong Word Dictionary*. He has been a technical writer, editor, and instructor for over 30 years. His experience includes commercial and government work for large corporations.

Before a career in written communications, Dave worked in radio syndication in Los Angeles, where he assisted in the production of nationally syndicated radio shows *American Top 40* and *American Country Countdown*.

In addition to being a senior member of the *Society for Technical Communication*, he also wrote two books on the late actor and champion bodybuilder Steve Reeves, titled *Steve Reeves – His Legacy in Films* and *Images of Steve Reeves*.

The author holds an M.S. from the University at Albany and a B.A. from the State University College at Potsdam. He lives in Saratoga Springs, New York.

Bibliography

The following *excellent* dictionaries and style guides were consulted in preparing this book:

American Century Dictionary. New York: Reissue. Warner Books, Incorporated, 1996.

American Heritage Dictionary of the English Language. 4th ed. New York: Houghton Mifflin Company, 2010.

Associated Press Stylebook and Libel Manual. Revised and Updated Edition. 43th ed. New York: Basic Books, 2009.

Chicago Manual of Style. 16th ed. Chicago: Univ. of Chicago Press, 2010.

Merriam-Webster's Collegiate Dictionary. 11th ed. Springfield, MA: Merriam-Webster, 2008.

Oxford American Desk Dictionary and Thesaurus. 3rd ed. New York: Berkley Publishing Group, 2010.

Random House Webster's College Dictionary. 3rd ed. New York: Random House, 2000

Random House Webster's Unabridged Dictionary. 2nd ed. New York: Random House, 2005

Webster's New World College Dictionary. 4th ed. New York: Wiley, John & Sons, Inc., 2004.

Webster's New World Roget's Thesaurus A-Z. 4th ed. New York: Wiley, John & Sons, Inc., 1999.

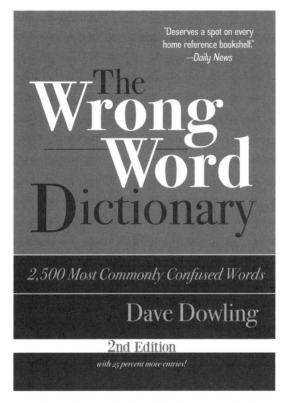